Writing for Public Relations

Writing for Public Relations

A Practical Guide for Professionals

Janet Mizrahi

BUSINESS EXPERT PRESS

Writing for Public Relations: A Practical Guide for Professionals

First published in 2016 by
Business Expert Press, LLC
222 East 46th Street, New York, NY 10017
www.businessexpertpress.com

ISBN-13: 978-1-63157-305-7 (paperback)
ISBN-13: 978-1-63157-306-4 (e-book)

Business Expert Press Corporate Communication Collection

Collection ISSN: 2156-8162 (print)
Collection ISSN: 2156-8170 (electronic)

Cover and interior design by Exeter Premedia Services Private Ltd., Chennai, India

First edition: 2016

10 9 8 7 6 5 4 3 2 1

Printed in the United States of America.

Abstract

The very nature of public relations—maintaining goodwill between an organization and its various stakeholders—requires a high degree of professionalism. This book examines the most common types of documents used in public relations and provides easy-to-follow descriptions of how to write them in a straightforward and effective manner.

Each chapter focuses on a specific type of document and includes helpful samples and useful checklists for writing:

- Daily correspondence
- News releases
- Newsletters
- Brochures
- Media kits
- Web copy
- Social Media

Students studying business, marketing, public relations, or communication as well as small business owners and employees will find this practical guide vital to their efforts to promote and inform various publics about their organizations.

Keywords

blog, brochure, e-newsletter, marcom, marketing, marketing style, media kit, microblog, news release, newsletter, pitch letter, press kit, press release, public relations, social media, Tweet, web copy, web writing, website, writing

Contents

Acknowledgments

I feel fortunate to have had two lives: one in the professional world, where I worked as a journalist and corporate communications writer; and the second as a college instructor, where I now pass along the knowledge I gained in my first career. This book is dedicated to the colleagues who have helped me along the way: the executives at the Los Angeles Daily News, with a special call-out to Debbie Gendel, my editor; my current co-workers at UCSB—you know who you are; and my always-available editor at BEP, Debbie DuFrene, a consummate professional.

I would also like to acknowledge the thousands of students I have taught. It is for you that I write these books. I hope they help you when you leave my classroom.

CHAPTER 1

Writing as a Public Relations Professional

Whether you are a student about to step into your first job in public relations or a more seasoned employee with years of experience, you must be able to communicate effectively to advance your career. Employers consistently rank good communication skills—speaking with customers and colleagues, presenting information, and writing—in the top tier of desired skills for both new hires and current employees. The ability to concisely and accurately convey meaning to different people is a prerequisite in today's fast-paced world, especially in a field such as public relations, which relies on communication.

Writing well as a professional whether the document is printed or on the screen is best taken on as a process, with careful attention paid to detail. This chapter will describe how to break down all writing tasks into a series of steps to streamline the process as well as describe the characteristics that all professional writing should embody.

Writing as a Process

Many people think that good writing flows out of the brain, into the fingers, and onto the page or screen. Nothing could be further from the truth. People who write professionally know that writing, like any acquired skill, requires patience and persistence. Whatever we are composing—anything from an e-mail message to a proposal for new business—the key to writing well is to consider writing a process rather than a one-shot deal. Your prose will be better and will take you less time to compose if you look at writing as a series of tasks. For those who suffer from writer's block or who shudder at the thought of writing, I can promise that if you break down writing into several component parts, the result will be better and you will feel less anxious.

The task of writing can be broken down into three separate steps, for which I have developed an acronym: AWE, short for Assess, Write, Edit. These three steps should be completed for every piece of writing that will be seen by another person. The only writing that doesn't require this process is personal writing.

Step 1: Assess. Before you ever put your fingers on the keyboard or put pen to paper, begin by assessing the writing situation and define your *audience and purpose.* I advise making this step formal: write down your answers.

Knowing the audience—your reader—is imperative for successful writing. Writers need to be very clear about the end user because the language and style we use depend upon who will read what we write. In essence, we have to psych out the reader to accomplish our writing goal. We cannot do that unless we analyze the reader accurately.

Define the characteristics of your reader as in Table 1.1. Begin the audience analysis portion of the first stage of the writing process (assessing) by completing an audience profile template, using the criteria in Table 1.1.

The next part of assessing the writing situation is defining your *purpose.* The reason or purpose for writing in the professional world falls into three basic categories: informing, persuading, or requesting. Informative writing is a large category that includes generalized information, instructions, notifications, warnings, or clarifications. Persuasive writing makes an impression, influences decisions, gains acceptance, sells, or recommends. Requests are written to gain information or rights and to stimulate action.

Unless you define the desired outcome of the written task, you cannot possibly achieve that task's objective. Are you writing an e-mail in response to a customer complaint? Are you using social media to generate traffic to a website selling nutritional supplements? You must be clear about what you want your words to accomplish before you write.

Sometimes you do not have all the information in hand that you need to write your document. Once you have defined for whom you are writing and what you want to accomplish, continue your analysis of the writing situation by gathering the information to produce the document. That may entail conducting *research.* Sometimes you may just need to

Table 1.1 Audience profile

Audience characteristic	Rationale
Age	Writing for children differs from writing for adults or teens. Your tone, word choice, and medium may differ greatly depending on the age of the reader.
Gender	Writing for an all-male audience will differ from writing for an all-female audience. Likewise, if the audience is mixed, you may make different language choices than you do for a homogeneous group.
Language proficiency	The reader's knowledge of English will affect your word choice, sentence length, and other stylistic elements.
Education level	You may be writing for an audience with a 10th grade reading level or one comprising college graduates. Each audience will have different expectations and needs, both of which you as the writer must be aware.
Attitude toward writer or organization	You must know if the audience is skeptical, frightened, pleased, or hostile toward you, the topic, or the organization. Anticipate your audience's reaction so you can write in a way that will support the document's purpose.
Knowledge of the topic	A document may be geared to people who are experts in a field or who know nothing about it. Even within an organization, several different audiences will exist. You may emphasize different aspects of a topic depending upon the readers' knowledge level.
Audience action	What do you want your audience to do after reading? Click a link for more information? Call to take advantage now? You must have a clear vision of your goal in communicating for your writing to be effective.

download information from your experience. Either way, have your information in hand *before* you begin to write. Nothing is more frustrating than being on a deadline to compose a writing job and realizing that you do not have the information you need.

This assessing portion of the writing process will make the actual writing much easier. Why? It is always easier to begin writing if you have something on the page rather than nothing.

Step 2: Write. Once you have the information, *organize* it. For shorter pieces, think about the organizational structure you need to follow to attain your writing purpose. For longer pieces, begin by creating categories of information. From these sections, draft an *outline* with headings.

Enter this second step of the writing process—writing an outline and a draft—knowing that it is not the last step. A draft by definition is not final. Its purpose is to transfer the information you have gathered onto the page. For short documents such as routine e-mails, consider composing offline. (It's too tempting to write and hit send without carefully going over your draft!) Begin the information you've gathered, making sure you include each point. For longer documents, use your outline. Write section by section, point by point. If you have trouble with one section, move to another.

Your goal at this stage of the writing process for both short and longer documents is to get something down on paper or on the screen that you will revise later. It's a waste of your valuable time to labor over any individual word or sentence as you write your draft; that word or sentence may be eliminated by the final version. If you cannot think of the precise word you need, leave a blank and return later to fill it in. If you are having difficulty wording a sentence smoothly, leave a bracketed space or perhaps type a few words as a reminder of the gist of what you want to say. The important point to remember is that a first draft is one of several stabs you'll take at this work.

If you write using information you have taken from other sources, avoid using someone else's words or ideas without attributing them. *Plagiarism* occurs when you use or closely imitate the ideas or language of another author without permission. Even if you paraphrase through rewording, you should still cite the source to avoid plagiarizing. With the abundance of material available to us with a few keystrokes, it's tempting to cut and paste and call it a day. But you leave yourself and your organization open to criminal liability for copyright infringement laws if you use words, images, or any other copyrighted material. Besides, you will never learn to express yourself if you use others' words.

Before you move to the next step, I advise printing your draft. But don't read it immediately. Let it marinate. It's too hard to edit your own copy immediately after you've written it. We need to let some time pass before we return to a draft so that we can be more objective when we edit.

Step 3: Edit. I saw a great t-shirt at a meeting for The Society for Technical Writers. On the front was the word *Write* in bold type. Following that was line after line of the word *Edit*. The final boldface word at the end of the last line was *Publish*. Of course, the idea is that writing requires more editing than writing.

Editing is a multistepped process and begins by looking at the overall effectiveness of the piece. As you read your draft, return to your audience and purpose analysis and ask yourself if the content meets the needs of the audience while it accomplishes your purpose in writing. Does the document provide all the information readers will need to do what you want? Does it make sense? Is it well organized? If not, go back and make changes.

Once you are certain that the content is correct and complete, it's time for *paragraph and sentence level editing*. This is where you'll need a good style guide (see discussion of Writing Tools) unless you are one of the few who have perfect recall of all grammatical rules. Begin by examining the effectiveness of each paragraph. By definition, a paragraph is a group of sentences about one topic; that topic is generally stated in the first sentence of a paragraph and is called a topic sentence. Good paragraphs have *unity*, which means they stay on topic, so first check each paragraph for unity. Make sure your paragraphs aren't too long. Long paragraphs scare readers off.

Next check your paragraphs for *cohesion*, meaning that each sentence leads logically to the next. A common writing error is to jump from one idea to the next without providing a logical connection between those two ideas. Unless each idea expressed in a sentence logically segues to the next, your reader will not be able to follow. Writers link ideas in several ways:

- Using transitional words and phrases. Transitions are broken down into types: adding information, contrasting information, comparing information, illustrating a point, and showing time.
- Using pronouns that refer back to a specific noun.
- Repeating key words to remind a reader of a central idea.

The following table illustrates the types of transitions writers use to compose cohesive sentences and paragraphs.

Table 1.2 Types of transitions

Type of transition	Words or phrases used
Additive—used to augment an idea	additionally, again, also, and, in addition, moreover, thus
Contrast—used to show how ideas differ	although, but, conversely, however, instead, on the other hand, yet
Comparison—used to link similar ideas	likewise, similarly
Time—used to show a sequence	after, finally, first, in the meantime, later, next, second, soon

Once all paragraphs are edited, examine each sentence. Now is the time to nitpick grammar and stylistic elements. Pay special attention to egregious errors such as:

- Subject–verb agreement
- Comma splices
- Sentence fragments
- Run-on sentences
- Dangling modifiers

Find every pronoun to make sure it agrees with its antecedent and that the noun to which it refers is clear. Make sure you have written numbers in the correct way, using numerals and spelling out numbers appropriately. Stay in the same verb tense. Also beware of dangling modifiers, phrases that confuse readers by saying something other than what is meant. They often appear in an introductory phrase at the beginning of a sentence but omit a word that would clarify meaning in the second part of the sentence. Look at the sentence below.

After finishing the copy, the website was difficult to understand.

The website did not finish the copy; therefore the meaning is obscured. Perhaps this sentence should have read:

After finishing the copy, the writer found that the website was difficult to understand.

As you edit, take some time to *read* your document *aloud* and make marks next to areas that require editing. This is the single best way to improve your writing. Professional writing should sound natural. If you find yourself stumbling as you read your copy, the chances are good that you have a problem; your ears will not allow you to pass over stylistic elements that your eye will just ignore.

As you speak your prose, listen for frequent repetition of the same word, for short, choppy sentences, and for sentences that begin with the same word or phrase. Make sure your sentences have variety in length, aiming for a good mix of short, medium, and longer sentences. Note whether you have started too many sentences with *there is, there are, this is,* or *it is.* Overuse of this wordy construction is a red alert for any professional writer to rewrite. Finally, make sure you have used words according to their actual definition, called the denotation. (Use the Avoiding Wordiness Checklist at the end of this chapter to help you edit for conciseness.)

The final element of the editing portion of the writing process is *proofreading.* Proofreading includes editing your copy for spelling, capitalization, punctuation, and typos. Begin by double-checking the correct spelling of names. Then make sure you've correctly used words that are commonly mistaken (i.e., affect/effect and complimentary/complementary). If you have included a phone number or a URL in the content, determine both are correct by phoning or checking the link.

A warning about using your word processor's spellcheck function: spellcheck is far from foolproof. Just the omission of one letter (say the last *s* in *possess*) can change the word's meaning, and the program won't pick that up. *Posses* is a word (the plural of posse) but it isn't the word you meant to use. Additionally, a spellchecker won't find names spelled incorrectly or words not in its dictionary.

Proofreading for punctuation is critical. Proper use of commas makes a huge difference in a document's readability. Be especially on the lookout for inserting commas after introductory phrases and between two independent clauses joined by a coordinate conjunction. Likewise, tossing in a comma or semicolon haphazardly and omitting a comma or semicolon are common writing errors that affect readability. Both can affect flow and meaning. Consider how the comma alters these two sentences:

> *That, I'm afraid, is not the case.*
> *That I'm afraid is not the case.*

The first sentence refers to a previous statement and conveys the meaning that an earlier statement is untrue. The second means that the individual claims to be unafraid.

Capitalization is another part of the proofreading stage. Use your style guide to know when to capitalize nouns and titles and be consistent. Next examine the appearance of what you've written. Remember that the copy must not only be well written; it must look attractive on the page or screen to maximize readability. You may find the Editing and Proofreading Checklist at the end of this chapter a helpful tool to guide you through this portion of the writing process.

Public Relations Writing Style

Writing for the world of work has certain characteristics that form the underpinning of anything you write, from an e-mail to your boss, to a resume for a new job, to a proposal for new business. Integrate the following elements into your work.

Accuracy. One of the best ways we can illustrate to our readers that we are professionals and experts is through accuracy. Inaccuracies show a carelessness that few professionals or organizations can afford in a competitive, global marketplace. Attention to accuracy is therefore paramount to professionals.

Active voice. To enliven your prose, avoid using passive voice construction when you can. Passive voice makes the object of an action the subject of a sentence, as the following example illustrates:

Passive Voice	*The e-mail was written by me.*
Active Voice	*I wrote the online blog.*

However, if you wish to obscure the person committing an action, you *should* use passive voice. Do so by not naming the actor, as is illustrated below:

Passive Voice	*The students were given poor grades.*
Active Voice	*The professor gave the students poor grades.*

If you have trouble identifying your own use of passive voice, you can adjust the Grammar Tools in Microsoft Word's Preferences, which when activated, will point out passive voice construction. If you are using passive voice purposefully because you want to sound objective, great. But if you have used passive voice unintentionally, change it.

Avoiding gender, racial, and age bias. English doesn't make biases easy to avoid. The best way to stay away from the he or she conundrum is to use the plural of a word. To avoid racial or age biases, beware of stereotypes when composing. Even if you feel the reference is complimentary, those to whom you refer may find that reference offensive.

Clarity. If a reader has to reread to understand anything you write, you have not done your job. Every sentence you write that another person will see should be easy to read. Clarity comes from using words the audience will recognize and using them correctly. Stay away from jargon or SAT-preparation vocabulary. One way to check your work for clarity is to give your draft to someone who knows nothing about what you are writing. If that reader can understand the document, it is probably clear.

Conciseness. Busy professionals are impatient and expect brevity. No one wants to wade through wordy prose to get to a point. As mentioned earlier, the Avoiding Wordiness Checklist at the end of this chapter contains some tips to make your writing more concise.

Conversational prose with smooth flow. The rhythm of any prose needs to be conversational and natural. The best way to achieve good flow is to read your document aloud and keep amending until you are able to read without hesitation. Use simple, plain language in sentences that are not complex or convoluted. Make sure your punctuation does not impede your reader by adding unnecessary halts or by avoiding pauses that will aid understanding.

To make your prose more conversational, you can also use contractions when appropriate. Instead of *they will*, use *they'll*. You can also begin your sentences with *and* or *but*, which many English teachers taught as an inviolable rule. Sometimes beginning a sentence with a conjunction gives prose just the right rhythm to create that highly desired conversational tone.

Correctness. Poor grammar and words used incorrectly make both the writer and the organization appear ignorant and sloppy. To hone your grammatical skills, work with a grammar guide next to you. (The use of writing tools is discussed later in this chapter.) Consult the guide when you are unsure about any writing issue. Make use of your word processor's grammar and spellcheck, but do not rely on them solely. Another way to work on grammar issues is to create a "Never Again" table. This is a three-column table (see Table 1.3) that lists a grammatical error, the rule that governs the problem, and a mnemonic device to remember the solution. When you keep a list of grammatical errors and refer to it as you compose, you will eventually learn to correct the problem. Keep adding and erasing errors until you no longer need to consult the chart.

Table 1.3 "Never again" table

Grammar problem	Rule	Mnemonic Device
Its versus It's	It's *always* = it is	The dog bites its tail because it's plagued with fleas.
Effect versus affect	Effect = noun Affect = verb	Ibuprofen adversely affects my stomach, but the medicine's effect cures my headache.

Parallelism. Good writing often uses a device called parallelism, or parallel structure. Writers use parallelism instinctually because it appeals to our natural desire for symmetry. Parallelism matches nouns with nouns, verbs with verbs, and phrases with phrases: "For *faster* action, *less* stomach upset, and *more* for your money, use XX." Readers expect parallelism, especially in sets of two or three items and in bulleted and enumerated lists. Using parallel phrasing correctly is key to professional writing.

Positive voice. Positive voice uses affirmative words to make a point. For example, instead of saying, "We are out of green t-shirts," we would emphasize the positive and say, "Order any size of our orange and gray t-shirts." Avoid downbeat words or words that can convey a negative connotation and rephrase in a positive way. Instead of, "No coupons will be honored after April 30," say, "Coupons will be honored through April 30."

Reliance on strong nouns and verbs. Good writing uses nouns and verbs to do the heavy work and saves adverbs and adjectives for rare occasions. Instead of "Our brightly-colored, twinkling lights will be reminders of the happiest, most memorable times you and your family will ever enjoy," say, "Our dazzling lights will twinkle their way into your family's memories." Replace "Our auto policies are competitive," with "Our auto policies beat the competitions." Avoid using the most boring and overused verb in the English language: to be. Check for overuse of *is, are, were*, and *was* and see if you can eliminate them by using a stronger, more specific verb. We can't entirely avoid adverbs or adjectives or "to be," but we can be mindful of how often we use them.

Sentence variety. Sentence variety is linked to conversational prose and has two elements. The first is sentence beginnings. As you edit, look at the way your sentences begin. Do three in a row begin with "The?" Do two sentences within two paragraphs begin with "There are?" Avoid writing sentences that begin with the same word or phrase. The second way to attain sentence variety is to vary sentence length. Short, choppy sentences make prose annoyingly staccato. Natural-sounding prose combines short, medium, and longer sentences.

One way to check your sentence length is to look at how the periods line up. If you see a vertical or slanted line of periods, you need to alter some of the sentence lengths. This can be accomplished in several ways. Join two sentences whose content is closely linked by embedding the gist of one sentence into another. Combine two sentences with a coordinate conjunction to create a complex sentence. Or try an alternate sentence beginning such as an introductory phrase, which will add sentence variety.

Simple words. Avoid jargon. Always, always, always choose the simpler, more recognizable word over the longer, more showy one. Instead of *rhinovirus* say *a cold*. Opt for *e-mail* over *electronic message*. In *utilize* versus *use, use* wins! (Notice how the number of words your reader has to wade through goes down with simpler words, too.)

Shorter paragraphs. Long paragraphs are appropriate for essays, but they have no place in professional documents. Big blocks of type scare readers away. The longest paragraph should be no more than six to eight lines. Always be aware of how a paragraph appears on a page (or a screen) and take pity on your audience—don't make your reader slog through dense prose.

Style: formal versus informal. Writers must wear different hats and adjust their writing style—sometimes called voice or tone—to the task at hand. In professional writing, we always aim for a natural style, as mentioned above. However, we must sometimes be even more specific about the style we choose.

Choosing to use an informal or formal writing style depends on the audience and the document's purpose. There is no clear-cut way to determine when to use each style; for example, sometimes an e-mail may require formality. Most of the time, however, e-mails are informal. To determine which style fits your needs, understand that informal writing allows the writer and reader to connect on a more personal level. It can convey warmth. Formal writing, on the other hand, produces the impression of objectivity and professionalism.

Some genres, however, have generally accepted styles. Use Table 1.4 to help guide you in choosing which style best suits your task.

Table 1.4 Formal and informal writing styles

	Formal style	Informal style
Types of documents	Letters Long reports Research Proposals	Most communication within the organization including e-mails, instant messages, memos, text messages Routine messages to outside audiences Informal reports
Characteristics	No personal pronouns (I, we) No contractions Objective voice or use of passive voice No figurative language or clichés No editorializing Limited use of adjectives No exclamation points Longer sentences Some technical language	Use of personal pronouns Use of contractions Shorter sentences, easily recognizable words Limited use of warm, inoffensive humor

Writing Tools

Just as a doctor wouldn't enter an examination room without a stethoscope or a carpenter wouldn't pull up to a job site without a hammer, no writer can be without the tools of the trade: a good dictionary, thesaurus, and style guide.

Many excellent writing reference books are on the market, both in electronic and print format. I use both. Although I often visit www.dictionary.com when I compose, I also rely on my hard copy dictionary. Dictionaries in book format allow us to browse, and sometimes you will chance upon a word or meaning; that doesn't happen when you use dictionary.com. The same goes for the thesaurus. I find the thesaurus built into Microsoft Word to be very weak. As a writer, I need to make the most out of the bounteous English language. A hard cover thesaurus is worth its weight in gold as far as I'm concerned. I use *Roget's 21st Century Thesaurus* edited by Barbara Ann Kipfer, PhD. I particularly like that it's organized like a dictionary.

Good style guides are likewise available. For a grammar guide, I use Diana Hacker's *A Writer's Reference*, 7th edition, but many excellent grammar reference books are available. Many good grammar websites can also be useful. The GrammarBook site (www.grammarbook.com/) and the Purdue Online Writing Lab (https://owl.english.purdue.edu/) offers handy and reliable ways to look up grammar issues you have.

The important thing to remember is to keep your tools nearby as you write. The more you use these reference books, the less you'll need them. You will internalize the rules of writing as you use them.

Conclusion

Writing well is a key to a successful career in public relations. By breaking down writing into stages called the writing process, your end product is more likely to accomplish its ultimate purpose. When composing on the job, effective writers integrate many elements that will distinguish their work as professional, well edited, and clear. Whether you choose hard copy or digital, use writing tools including a dictionary, thesaurus, and grammar guide to create professional documents. Doing so will help you excel and exude the professionalism so necessary in public relations.

Avoiding wordiness checklist

Wordy phrase and example	Solution	√
Avoid beginning a sentence with *There are* or *It is.* *There are four points that should be considered.* *It is clear that cashmere is warmer.*	Begin sentences with the true subject. *Consider these four points* or *Four points should be considered.* *Cashmere is clearly warmer.*	
Avoid beginning sentences with *That* or *This.* *Choosing teams should be done carefully. This is because a good mix will generate better results.*	Connect to previous sentence. *Choosing teams should be done carefully because a good mix will generate better results.*	
Use *active voice* rather than passive. *Rain forests are being destroyed by uncontrolled logging.*	Passive voice depletes prose of vitality and can almost always be rewritten in active voice. *Uncontrolled logging is destroying rain forests.*	
Omit *that* or *which* whenever possible. *The water heater that you install will last 15–20 years.*	Unless *that* or *which* is required for clarity, omit. *The water heater you install will last 15–20 years.*	
Avoid prepositional phrase modifiers. *The committee of financial leaders meets every Tuesday.*	Replace with one-word modifiers. *The financial leaders committee meets every Tuesday.*	
Avoid *be* verbs *New Orleans is one of the most vibrant cities in the U.S.*	Replace with a strong verb. *New Orleans vibrates with activity like no other U.S. city.*	
Tighten closely related sentences of explanation. *When hanging wallpaper, three factors need to be considered. The factors are X, X, and X.*	Join closely related sentences of explanation with a colon to avoid repetitions. *When hanging wallpaper, consider three factors: X, X, and X.*	
Tighten closely related sentences. *MRIs are used to diagnose many ailments. MRIs create an image of organs and soft tissues to diagnose.*	Omit repetitious phrasing in the second sentence. *MRIs diagnose many ailments by creating images of organs and soft tissues.*	

(Continued)

Avoiding wordiness checklist (Continued)

Wordy phrase and example	Solution	√
Tighten verb phrases with auxiliary + ing verbs *Management was holding a staff meeting.*	Replace *is, are, was, were, or have* + verb with a one-word verb. *Management held a staff meeting.*	
Avoid using *there is or there are* within a sentence. *When creating a mail list, there are many pitfalls.*	Find an active verb to replace *there is or there are.* *When creating a mail list, many pitfalls exist.*	
Remove redundancies. *An anonymous stranger may be dangerous.*	Know the true meaning of a word. *Strangers may be dangerous.*	

Editing and proofreading checklist

Item	✓
Document content is tailored to meet needs of audience and attains writing purpose	✓
Copy is edited for conciseness	✓
Body paragraphs have unity and cohesion and are shortened for visual appeal	✓
Transitions in and between paragraphs adequately link ideas	✓
Grammar is correct	✓
Punctuation is used correctly	✓
Copy has good rhythm and flow and uses a natural and conversational tone	✓
Sentences show variety in beginning and length	✓
Names are spelled correctly; phone numbers and URLs are accurate	✓
Words are used correctly	✓
Capitalization is consistent and adheres to specific stylebook guidelines	✓
Document adheres to specific genre formatting guidelines	✓
Document shows professionalism	✓

CHAPTER 2

Routine Communication

Much of the communication you are called upon to write in public relations will entail delivering routine messages such as requests for information or action, replies to customers, and explanations of events or systems. Goodwill messages—used to build relationships and extend warmth—are also a common type of routine message.

Routine messages are considered positive in situations when the reader will be pleased, interested, or feel neutral about the message. For example, if you were writing to a customer to confirm a meeting date, the recipient would likely be pleased or at the very least feel neutral about the message. Similarly, if you were writing to congratulate a colleague about a promotion, the reader's reaction would be to feel pleased. The audience's expected response to any message dictates how that message is written. Positive messages are organized using a *direct approach*, which is constructed using three elements:

1. Opening stating the main purpose, subject, or idea
2. Body containing relevant details explaining the subject
3. Ending with a polite request, summary, or goodwill thought

We will discuss how this organizational strategy manifests itself in specific genres later in this chapter.

The way you relay a positive or routine message—in other words, the type of media you select to transmit the message—depends on several factors. In some situations, your company may dictate communication protocol, in which case you must adhere to those guidelines. However, other times you may need to choose from the various types of media: e-mail, letter, memo, phone, or text message. Your choice will depend upon your audience, the level of formality the situation calls for, and your purpose in writing.

Table 2.1 offers you help in deciding which media (also referred to as a "channel") to choose for various routine messages.

Table 2.1 Media communication channels

Media type	When to use
E-mail	For routine communication 24/7 that may not require immediate attention; used between co-workers in an organization and to outside stakeholders
Instant messaging	To receive immediate feedback from a co-worker who is also online; also used in customer–vendor "chats"
Letter	For formal written documentation, especially with individuals outside of the organization
Memo	To present information, policies, procedures within an organization
Text messaging	To leave short messages that may or may not be seen immediately by co-workers; also for some marketing messages to customers
Phone: direct conversation	For immediate feedback; to connect personally; in lieu of face-to-face meeting
Voice-mail message	To leave routine or important information (not highly sensitive in nature)

Whichever channel you use, remember that all professional communication must adhere to the professional writing characteristics we discussed in Chapter 1.

Writing Routine Messages

Each of the above media has specific characteristics. Here we will discuss the elements of most widely used written genres for routine and positive messages; sample documents of genres appear in the Appendix.

E-mail

As a genre, e-mail is entrenched in the modern workplace. A recent survey found that workers look at their inboxes an average of 74 times a day.[1] Although text messages and video chats have replaced some e-mail, it is still an integral part of writing for public relations.

In general, e-mail is used to exchange information with clients and colleagues any time of the day or night.[2] While that makes e-mail convenient for both the reader and the writer, it also means your message may not be read or responded to immediately. Therefore, e-mail should not be used for urgent issues. Some say e-mail is most appropriate for short messages that require a response to an inquiry or that ask for information.[3] However, it is not uncommon to see longer e-mails that deal with more complex issues. Likewise, e-mails often act as replacements for traditional letters or memos. E-mail is also used when several or many people must view the same message.

All e-mails contain basic elements you should incorporate into short, long, formal, or informal messages, as outlined in the following discussion.

Subject Line. An e-mail's subject line accurately and succinctly reflects the message's content. Working people are busy and their e-mail inboxes are packed with dozens or even hundreds of messages to sift through. Writing subject lines with specific wording that clearly identifies the topic will help your reader. Notice how the vague subject line below leaves the reader wondering, while the specific subject line leaves little to the imagination.

Vague subject line　　　*New Policy*
Specific subject line　　*New Branding Policy Effective June 1*

When writing your subject line, avoid inflated or emotional appeals such as "Urgent" or "Critical Situation." (If a situation is truly critical, you should probably phone the individual instead of sending an e-mail!) Also be aware of ethical choices when writing a subject line and don't make claims that are misleading or untrue. While it may be tempting to lure a reader into an e-mail by using a catchy subject line like "Free Subscription!" unless you are actually offering a free subscription, you are misleading readers who will not appreciate being lured into a disingenuous e-mail that wastes their valuable time.

Greeting or Salutation. A greeting at the beginning of an e-mail is a visual cue that shows the recipient where to start reading. The type of greeting or salutation in an e-mail depends on the recipient and the level of formality required by the situation. Writing to an outside

audience—those not in your organization—is usually a more formal situation, so use a person's title (Mr., Ms., Mrs., Dr., Prof.) until that individual replies using a first name. Once you are on a first name basis, you
can tone down the level of formality and write "Dear Brad." You can also
wrap the salutation into the first line of your e-mail as is shown below:

Thanks, Brad, for the information about the geothermic survey.

For less formal situations, use one of the below salutations:

> *Hi, Brad,*
> *Brad,*
> *Hello, Brad,*
> *Good morning, Brad,*

If a discussion thread—a series of e-mails on the same topic—is ongoing, you may find that a greeting becomes unnecessary. This is a common
practice, but only after the thread of the conversation has gone on for
several more formal e-mails.

Finally, addressing a group differs from addressing individuals. If
sending an e-mail blast to a list of customers, for example, you may
want to choose a greeting such as "Dear Valued Customer." If sending an
e-mail to a committee, it is appropriate to begin the correspondence with
the committee's name, as noted below.

Dear Land Assessment Committee:

Avoid using the generic "To Whom It May Concern." Use of this
greeting in an e-mail shows you haven't done your homework.[4] If an
e-mail is replacing a traditional letter, use a standard letter salutation,[5]
which we will discuss later in this chapter.

Opening. The first paragraph of e-mails delivering routine news or
information should contain an expanded explanation of the topic mentioned in the subject line. For example, the opening for an e-mail about
the new branding policy we mentioned earlier would begin by frontload-
ing the first paragraph and elaborating on the subject.

Direct opening: *A new policy for using branding on all written
material will take effect on Monday, June 1, 2017.*

Restating the purpose of the e-mail in the first paragraph helps busy readers who may have skipped the subject line or who want to know exactly what they are reading about. Avoid indirect first paragraphs such as the one below, which unnecessarily take up your readers' time.

Wordy indirect opening: *The recent problems we have had with mix-ups about when to use the new branding has resulted in management instituting a new policy to take effect June 1, 2017.*

Body. The body of your e-mail contains the details required to fully understand the topic stated in both the subject line and opening. It should be written in short paragraphs of no more than six to eight lines and no more than 60 to 70 characters across (a character is a letter, punctuation, or a space). In the body of the e-mail, use graphical markers, headings, white space, and bulleted or enumerated points to break up text and make reading both short and long e-mails easier.

To avoid confusion, restrict each e-mail to one topic. Though it may seem counterintuitive, sending several consecutive e-mails to the same person, each covering one topic, will be more effective than trying to deal with too much in one e-mail for several reasons. First, many people do not read carefully and only focus on the beginning of the e-mail, scanning the rest. Second, receiving several e-mails with different subject lines allows your reader to pick which e-mail to respond to first. Finally, individually labeled e-mails, identified by specific subject lines, help the sender, too. If you have sent one person several e-mails on different topics, you will be happy to receive a reply to each item rather than having to wade through one dense, long response.

Closing. A final paragraph, statement, or phrase that closes the e-mail helps readers understand what to do next or tells them that they have reached the end of the correspondence. End routine news by using one of these options:

- **Action information, dates, deadlines**. When you want readers to take an action, provide the information they need to do so. Assign an end date and time.

- **Summary of message**. In longer messages, you may want to recap the main points covered in the message.
- **Polite closing thought**. Express gratitude or encourage feedback, but avoid clichés such as "Please do not hesitate to call for further information."[6]

A closing helps avoid an abrupt, curt-sounding ending to your e-mail. Short closings such as "See you next week," "All the best," and "Warm regards" are less formal and are perfect for e-mails to co-workers or those with whom you have developed a cordial work relationship.

Signature Block. Always include your name at the end of any e-mail. Because e-mails are not written on letterhead, a signature block is used to provide contact information. E-mail applications contain options for using several different signature blocks. Formal e-mails—those going to outside vendors or customers or from an organizational leader to the staff—should contain complete contact information as is illustrated below.

Full Name and Title	*Caroline Johnson, Design Manager*
Organization Department	*Creative Services*
Organization Name	*Mentor, Inc.*
Mailing Address	*3366 Broad Street, Portland, OR 97205*
Phone	*503-877-9000 ext. 27*
	Fax: 503-977-9300
Web Address	*www.mentor.com*

Less formal e-mails may contain modified signature blocks with less information or the addition of an extra line with the writer's first name, as shown below.

Best,
Carrie
Caroline Johnson, Design Manager
Creative Services

Tone. Because e-mail doesn't allow the reader to see body language or facial cues, hitting the right tone can be difficult. You may send an e-mail you consider to the point and concise, but your reader may consider it abrupt or terse. Likewise, you may insert a humorous tidbit that your reader finds silly or even offensive.

The best way to avoid being misunderstood is to be polite.[7] Reread your e-mail before you send it. If it sounds too blunt, add a "please" or "thank you" or acknowledge the individual on a personal level. Never use sarcasm, and be wary of humor. Peoples' definitions of what is funny differ greatly.

Another point: Do not use emoticons such as emojis in professional e-mails. If you need a facial expression to soften or add meaning to your words, your words are not properly chosen.

Document Design. To make your e-mails readable, follow these formatting guidelines.

- Limit length of lines to 60 to 70 characters.
- Keep paragraph length to six to eight lines maximum.
- Use left justified, ragged right margins.
- Use single spacing for paragraphs, double spacing between paragraphs.
- Employ graphical devices such as headings, white space, or bullets, or enumeration as appropriate.
- Include signature block.

Short e-mails (up to one screen) may not require headings. However, the longer the e-mail, the more important it is to break up the text into clearly identifiable sections marked by well-written headings. Refer to the Appendix for a sample e-mail.

E-mail Etiquette and Best Practices

A major complaint among people in the workforce is that e-mail clogs their inboxes and drains their time. One study found that the average employee in a corporation will spend more than one-fourth of each day dedicated to sending and reading e-mail and will receive more than 115 messages.[8] To help your e-mails gain your reader's attention, be aware of these best practices, sometimes called "netiquette," for e-mail use.

Table 2.2 E-mail best practices or netiquette

Limit e-mails to one topic.
Send e-mail only to those who must receive the information; use "cc" and "reply all" sparingly to reduce e-mail overload.
Use "bcc" (blind carbon copy) to send mass mailings so all e-mail addresses are not visible to the entire list of recipients; do not use "bcc" to send sensitive information.
Always include a clear subject line; change subject line when a discussion thread switches topic.
Never send an e-mail when angry (called "flaming").
Avoid forwarding jokes, spam, or off-color remarks when using company devices.
Use a professional sounding e-mail address.
Be concise and get to the point quickly.
Hit the right level of formality. If you use a person's first name in person, use the first name in an e-mail. If you do not know a person, begin by using a title ("Hello, Ms. Chen").
Never send an e-mail asking for information that has already been provided. It makes you look lazy or inattentive to detail.
Employ white space, headings, bullets, and short paragraphs to enhance readability.
Reply to e-mails within 24 hours, even if just to say you've received the message and will deal with it at a later date.
Edit carefully. Typos, misspellings, and grammatical errors undermine your credibility. Spell out rather than using abbreviations.
Mention attached documents in the body of the e-mail and make sure you have actually attached them.

Letters

Letters are the preferred channel for documents that require a written record, especially when communicating with associations, the government, and customers. Print letters are also used in resignations and for recommendations. The benefit of a printed letter with a handwritten signature is that it conveys authority, formality, respect, and importance. Letters also stand out among the sea of e-mails most people receive daily.

When writing a letter whose purpose is to provide routine information or news or to request without using persuasion, use the direct approach outlined earlier. Whether you include a subject line or not, begin routine news letters with a direct statement of the letter's purpose, as shown below:

> *It is with great pleasure that I write this recommendation for Kirsten Talbot, with whom I had the pleasure of working for three years.*

> *We would be delighted to visit your tenth grade students to discuss the field of public relations on Thursday, July 17, as you requested.*

Letters contain the following mandatory elements.

Letterhead. All letters should be written on letterhead stationery that includes the full address and contact information of the organization or the individual. Most organizations will have letterhead in both hard copy and electronic versions.

Date. The date the letter is being written should use no abbreviations (i.e., January 16, 2015, *not* Jan. 16, 2015). Ordinals are *never* used in the date (1st, 2nd, 3rd, 24th, etc.).

Inside Address. The inside address contains the name and address of the person receiving the letter. The name should be preceded by a title (Mr., Ms., etc.). In today's workplace, it is common to refer to a woman as *Ms.* unless she has shown a preference for *Miss* or *Mrs.* Use professional titles (Dr., Professor, Senator) over generic titles. If sending a letter to someone in an organization, include the person's title under the name, followed by the name of the organization and its address:

> *Ms. Jeanine Bauer*
> *Public Relations Manager*
> *Tri County Area Governments*
> *232 South El Sueño Road*
> *Santa Teresa, CA 93115*

Salutation. Letters call for a formal salutation followed by a colon. If addressing a letter to an individual, write:

Dear Ms. Bauer:

If addressing two people, use:

Dear Ms. Bauer and Mr. Gresham:

When addressing a group, use a collective name such as Committee, Members, Customers, and so on:

Dear Hiring Committee:
Dear Valued Members:
Dear Loyal Customers:

Only include the first and last name in a salutation if you are sending a letter to someone you do not know and the name is of ambiguous gender, such as *Pat Saunders* or *Chris Terlikian.*

Subject Line. Although not essential, some people add an informative subject line that foretells the letter's purpose and key facts,[9] such as this:

Subject: Classroom Visit to Mercury Public Relations on July 17

Body. The detail of the letter's message is considered the body. It should conform to the rules of effective professional communication that we've previously discussed: use of short paragraphs, bullets, headings (if appropriate), and white space to make a letter attractive and easy to read.

Complimentary Closing. The most traditional way to sign off a letter is with a complimentary closing such as *Sincerely* or *Cordially* followed by a comma. *Thank you* or *Best wishes* followed by a comma may be used for less formal letters.

Signature Block. The sender's signature block follows the complimentary close. Allow three to four spaces for the handwritten signature, and type the sender's full name and title. Sign the full name (first and last) for formal letters, and the first name only for less formal letters. Do not include the address of the organization; doing so on letterhead would be redundant.

End Notes. Sometimes a business letter requires a notation, the last element on the page that comes two lines after the signature block. These include reference initials, enclosures, or copy notices. Reference initials are the typist's initials after the sender's. For example, say Jorge M. Marquez is sending the letter but his assistant, Leslie Adler, typed it. The reference initials would be: JMM:la or JMM/la.

Whenever a letter contains something besides the letter, notify the reader with the notation *Enclosure* or *Enc*. If more than one enclosure is contained, the notation should indicate so: Enclosure (3).

If anyone else is receiving a copy of a letter, indicate that with the notation *c: John Doe.*

Letter Document Design. Some organizations have their own guidelines for letter design, which you must follow. Otherwise, the most common style for letters is the *block style*. Block style conforms to the following parameters:

- Left align, ragged right
- No paragraph tabs
- Single spacing
- Double spacing between paragraphs

Other letter designs are modified block, in which the date, complimentary closing, and signature block are aligned about midway across the page. Whichever design you are using, always check the appearance of your letter in the preview mode of your word processing program. A letter should not be crammed into the top of the page; it should look balanced. If your letter is short, increase your margins and use a slightly larger font size. To help balance on the page, add white space above and below the date.

Your letter will have to go inside an envelope. Most word processing applications have an envelope function that allows you to type the return address (unnecessary if you are using a company envelope with pre-printed return address) and the address. Never send a typed letter in a handwritten envelope. If your letter is handwritten, however, a neatly handwritten envelope is acceptable.

Refer to the Appendix for a sample letter.

Memos

Memos (or memoranda) are documents written to audiences within organizations. They can be as short as one page or much longer and are used in situations that require a permanent or formal record. Types of memos include short reports, proposals, or other informational correspondence. Sometimes memos are printed; other times, they are sent as an attachment to an e-mail.

The writing strategy for routine memos is the same as that used in routine e-mails and letters. Begin with the purpose of the memo; use the body paragraphs to provide any details or explanations to support the main point; end with a forward looking closing that either summarizes the message (*We are certain that these new procedures will result in improved workflow.*), asks for an action with an end date (*Please turn in your expense reports on the first working day of each month beginning in February.*), or offers a polite, concluding thought (*I am looking forward to completing the project and for your feedback on our work to date.*).

Memo Document Design. Memos are generally written on stationery with the organization's name on top. Full letterhead is unnecessary because the memo is going to an internal audience. Under the company name, the word Memo or Memorandum is typically centered. On the left margin, use boldfaced guidewords *Date:, To:, From:, Subject:*.

Be sure to use the tab to align the information following the guidewords. Skip three lines and then begin the memo. Use graphical devices such as headings, bulleted or enumerated points, and white space to break up text and to guide your reader. If a memo is longer than one page, number the pages. And of course, memos do not need to be signed, since the sender's name appears in the guidewords. However, you may write in your initials next to your name in the "From" line.

Refer to the Appendix for a sample memo.

Text Messaging

The popularity of text messaging with smart phones has no doubt impacted every aspect of our lives, including the workplace. Today text messages have replaced some phone calls and e-mails for transmitting short messages in both large and small organizations.

Like e-mail, text messages should be used to transmit nonsensitive information. For example, it is perfectly acceptable to use a text message to notify a customer that an order has arrived. It is not acceptable to resign from a job in a text.

If you are texting for work-related reasons, always follow company policies. If none have been established, ask your supervisor about the types of situations in which texting would be acceptable. Note that while it is common for texting between friends to use shorthand, emoticons, abbreviations, and lack of attention to grammar, such practices have *no* place on the job. Doing so shows a lack of professionalism that will not earn you respect.

Keep in mind the following points when texting for work.

- Never text sensitive or confidential material.
- Keep text messages brief.
- Use proper grammar and spelling.
- Avoid texting while speaking to someone.
- Identify yourself if texting someone you don't know.

Types of Routine Messages

Various situations that arise in work settings call for specific types of routine messages. The choice of how these messages is delivered—whether via e-mail, letter, memo, or text—depends on the organization and situation. Consider the following explanations of the types of routine messages you may encounter in the workplace and details about how they are composed.

Requests and Responses

Making and responding to requests comprise a good deal of the types of messages you will be called upon to write. These types of routine messages are straightforward and call for the direct strategy. When writing routine requests, follow the following formula.

1. State the request directly in a polite, undemanding tone.
2. Provide details that explain the request, asking questions if necessary. Be sure you include all the information the reader will need to be able to respond adequately to your request. Whenever possible, add reader benefits—*Completing the form will allow us to process your invoice quickly*—to add the likelihood of a response.
3. End with a request for a specific action and show appreciation.

Replies or responses to requests should also use the direct strategy:

1. Respond directly to the inquiry in the opening.
2. Answer all questions in the body.
3. Encourage a positive response, if appropriate, or end with a polite goodwill statement.

Appreciation or Goodwill

Relationship building is an important aspect of anyone's career and is especially valuable to those in the public relations field. Sending goodwill messages to colleagues, employees, clients, customers, or others shows that you are an empathetic and thoughtful individual. It also helps build relationships, key in public relations.

Show appreciation by sending a thank-you message when you receive a gift or experience hospitality. Write a goodwill message to acknowledge the receipt of an award, to recognize a job well done, or a promotion. Handwritten notes are the most personal way to express thanks and can be written on company letterhead or on elegant, simple stationery. Situations calling for a more businesslike goodwill message are best sent in an e-mail or a letter.

Use the direct strategy for appreciation or goodwill messages. Begin with the main point:

Thank you for opening your beautiful home to our staff for the annual company holiday party.

Congratulations on the birth of your new daughter, Sarah Ann! As a father myself, I know the joys awaiting you and Maureen.

Our staff has been eagerly implementing the new time saving techniques you presented in your recent workshop.

Include specific details about the situation in the body to show you are writing more than a generic thank-you and avoid overblown, exaggerated claims.

Most noteworthy, the public relations department has already decreased its IT service requests by 20 percent due to the new system you created.

Not

The staff has been amazed by how much time they are already saving because of your awesome system!

End with sincere words and avoid clichés such as *Best luck in the future*. Send goodwill messages in a timely manner and keep them short.

Negative Messages

Delivering unwanted news is a fact of life in public relations, and when an organization must inform its stakeholders of negative news, there are basic goals that the message must attain:

- Confirm that the negative message will be understood and accepted.
- Deliver the message in a way that the reader will continue to look at the writer and/or organization in a positive light.
- Minimize future contact with the writer/organization about the negative situation.

In some cases, delivering negative news uses the direct strategy. For example, anyone who has ever received a rejection letter from a college (certainly unwanted news!) knows that the negative message came in the first line. This was done so that the anxious student did not overlook the information. If you think your reader would prefer to read the negative news first or if the situation demands firmness, use the direct approach. Begin with the negative news itself, explain the reasons for the negative news in the body, and close politely but firmly.

However, negative messages are frequently delivered using the indirect strategy. This structure has four main elements, as Table 2.3 illustrates.

Table 2.3 Indirect strategy elements

Indirect strategy elements	Writing strategy
Neutral or buffer statement	Describe a point on which both parties can agree Express appreciation Begin with good news Offer praise
Reasons leading to message	Include details supporting the denial Omit apologizing Use positive language wherever possible
The negative or undesired news	Clearly state the bad news so to eliminate any misunderstanding Deemphasize the bad news by placing it in a subordinate clause
Polite close	Aim to build goodwill by offering an alternative, if possible, or a simple forward-looking statement

Begin your negative message with a **buffer or neutral statement** about which both the writer and reader can agree. Say your firm is handling the public relations for a club that is also used as a venue, and you must deliver negative news to an inquiry. A buffer could be written thus:

> *The recent renovation of the University Club has made it a much sought-after venue.*

Alternately, you may wish to start with a statement of **appreciation:**

> *Thank you for your well researched proposal to include Mayweather House in this year's Giving Back!® volunteer day.*

You can offer any **positive news** that is part of the message (as long as it does not mislead the reader into thinking the message contains all positive news) or offer praise to open your negative news message:

> *All departments have done a great job in decreasing their operating budgets.*

Start the second paragraph of the negative message by providing logical **reasons** leading to the bad news itself. Slip in the **negative news** in a subordinate clause, and never repeat it. Be sure the negative message is clearly stated so you do not create misunderstanding or encourage further communication. For example, going off the buffer statement made earlier, our next sentence might read:

Since we have expanded our facility to accommodate parties of over 100 and added a gourmet chef, the number of organizations and individuals requesting to use the University Club for events has tripled. Our bylaws require that we give priority to members of the club before opening up our schedule to non-members, so we are unable to accommodate your request to use the Dean's Room on the date you have requested.

The **closing** of the negative message must be polite and promote goodwill to the reader, who has just heard unwelcome news. Avoid being too conciliatory by offering to provide "additional assistance" or to "call us if you have further questions." If you are able to offer an alternative, do so. For example, if you know that another facility is available to accommodate the above-mentioned University Club event or you can hold it on a different day, say so. If not, simply end on a positive note:

Thank you for considering the University Club for your event, and we look forward to helping you in the future.

Refer to the Appendix for an example of a negative news message.

Conclusion

Much of your day-to-day writing will be routine and will therefore conform to a direct writing strategy. There are many types of routine messages including requests, responses, claims, adjustments, and goodwill. Choosing the right channel for routine messages—e-mail, letter, memo, or texting—depends on the urgency and formality of the message itself. These everyday messages require a high degree of clarity and conciseness and therefore can be surprisingly challenging to write.

CHAPTER 3

Writing News Releases

The news release is probably the most common type of writing a public relations professional will be called upon to create. A news release—also widely referred to as a press release—is an organization's message written to appeal to news media outlets in hopes that those outlets will disseminate the message. News releases contain information the organization wants to publicize or "release." That message can take many forms. It may be news about a recent hire, an employee's promotion, a product, or an event the company is sponsoring. News releases are often used to put a company's spin on bad news about earnings, product problems, or other events that reflect negatively on an organization. Both nonprofit and for-profit groups routinely use this form of communication.

However, the Internet has created an entirely new purpose for news releases. Today organizations issue news releases intended solely for their stakeholders. These releases are uploaded to a company's website and reside there to communicate company news to interested parties.

Because many news releases are written with an eye toward the media, it is important to understand how the media—both traditional and new—use news releases. Traditional or "legacy" media, that is, broadcasters, digital news outlets, newspapers, and trade and consumer magazines, either cover a geographic area (think *Detroit Free Press*) or are designed to appeal to a specific niche (e.g., Lifetime Network, *Sports Illustrated*, or *Grammarly.com*). In traditional media, news is gathered when reporters go to a scene of an incident (city hall, an accident scene, a new play, a sporting event), uncover facts, and report them. In new media, a blogger may be following a particular topic and use a news release for background information.

Whether it's the *Miami Herald*, CNBC, or a blog, which stories run is up to the publisher or editor. In newspapers, editors decide if news appears on the front page or is buried in the middle of the business section. On-air editors choose their lead news story and then allocate time to other features for television or radio broadcasts. Bloggers cull the web looking for interesting trends or some reason to publicize news, whether that is coupons, free tickets or products, or a unique idea. The news release provides these media with story ideas they may otherwise ignore. Because media representatives are busy and do not want to give a business free publicity, savvy news releases will be well-written, factual, and accurate news that will be of interest to the media's readers or viewers.

Types of Releases

Most news releases contain up-to-the-minute news and are generally serious in nature. Although all types of news releases contain the same general elements, they are used to promote varying objectives. The following are commonly used types of news releases:

- **Publicity release**. This type of release announces information about a business, organization, product, or service that has news value to local or national media. A publicity release may announce internal promotions, upcoming or past events, new hires or appointments, awards, honors, and mergers or acquisitions.
- **Product release**. These releases contain information that is generally targeted at trade publications and relate news about the introduction of a product, an addition to a line, or a modification or improvement to an existing product.
- **Bad news release**. When an organization must tell the truth about a negative situation, it issues a bad news release. This document must always be straightforward about the negative news, providing facts in an honest, forthright fashion to establish credibility.
- **Financial release**. The financial release disseminates information about a company's earnings or other information of interest to shareholders. Although national media such as the *Wall Street Journal* or *ABC Nightly News* may be interested in reporting news about large, publicly held organizations, local

media also tend to report on firms headquartered in their distribution area.

- **Feature release**. Sometimes an organization may wish to send a news entity a fully developed story that is neither late-breaking news or serious. These kinds of stories are called features or "soft news" and require a different style than other releases. A feature release is not always timely; in fact, feature releases can often be used any time and are therefore called "evergreen." They are more creative than hard news releases and contain an idea for a feature story or the story in its entirety.

Most news releases emulate traditional journalistic news articles and contain *news values*, or the five Ws and one H, as shown in Table 3.1.

Table 3.1 News values

News value	Definition
Who	Exact names and titles of people involved
What	Major action or news; often includes lesser actions or supporting facts related to major news
When	Time of news clearly stated
Where	Location of where news occurred or will occur
Why or How	Explanation of news including its context

News releases must be *newsworthy* to appeal to the media. Table 3.2 illustrates elements or *angles* that emphasize newsworthiness.

Table 3.2 Elements of newsworthiness

Newsworthy element	Explanation
Timeliness	Refers to an event or news that just happened or will happen
Prominence	Appeals to public's interest in prominent figures and celebrities
Proximity	Ties a local angle to a larger story
Significance	Affects a significant number of people or greatly affects some person or subset of people
Newness	Generates interest with mention of "free" and "new"

News Release Format

News releases follow a predictable format and include specific elements, as outlined below.

Letterhead. News releases often appear on the organization's *letterhead* stationery. At the very least, the group's logo should appear at the top.

Headline ("head") and subhead. A headline ("head") concisely captures the main idea of the release. Headlines are written with present-tense verbs and frequently omit the articles "a," "an," and "the." The headline in a news release is crucial because if it does not clearly appeal to the reader and get the message across quickly, the release will be ignored. The headline is, in essence, the "sales pitch," although it must be worded to avoid sounding like an advertisement. Consider the difference in these two headlines. The first is overly persuasive, and the second is more objective.

New Herb Guarantees Safe Weight Loss and Money-Back Guarantee

New Study Shows Herb's Effectiveness as Weight Loss Tool

An effective headline uses clear, concrete language, and avoids vague, unspecific words. It should not contain the same wording as the lead paragraph, although it will contain the main idea of the release. For best search engine optimization (SEO), the headline should contain key words that are repeated strategically throughout the release and that echo the essence of the message. Many experts say that headlines today should be written for social sharing networks, and consequently, should be limited to 80 to 100 characters.[1] However, it is not uncommon to see long headlines that communicate the main point of the release. The following are examples of a long and a more tightly worded headline.

Coca-Cola Enterprises, Coca-Cola Iberian Partners and Coca-Cola Erfrischungsgetränke AG to Form Coca-Cola European Partners

Coca-Cola Releases 2014/2015 Sustainability Report

Subhead. A subhead is not mandatory, but if used, its purpose is to add another layer of information to the headline. A subhead provides details omitted in the headline and is written in a complete sentence.

Dateline. A dateline is the location of the city from which the release is issued written in capitals followed by the date of the release. The following is an example of a dateline:

SACRAMENTO, CA.,--January 21, 2017

Lead. A news release's first paragraph is called a lead. *Summary leads* are a tersely worded synopsis of the main point and include some or all of the journalistic news values of who, what, where, and when. A *delayed lead* is used for a more dramatic opening or for a feature news release. The headline and lead echo the same information but do not use the same words to state it. Leads are often long to integrate more news value into the first paragraph. Note the length of this lead from a Bank of America press release, which answers the *who, what,* and *when.*

> *The world's top professional wheelchair athletes will go head-to-head in the first Chicago-New York Challenge, it was announced today by Carey Pinkowski, executive race director of the Bank of America Chicago Marathon and Peter Ciaccia, president of events for New York Road Runners and race director of the TCS New York City Marathon.*[2]

Body. The body of the news release is a series of short paragraphs that come directly after the lead. The body is written using the inverted pyramid style of organization (see Figure 3.1), listing points to further explain

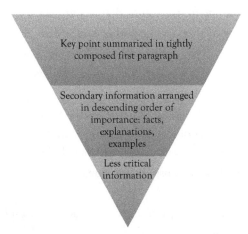

Key point summarized in tightly composed first paragraph

Secondary information arranged in descending order of importance: facts, explanations, examples

Less critical information

Figure 3.1 Inverted pyramid organizational style

the news lead in descending order of importance. The body covers the why and(or) the how. News release body paragraphs may include bulleted points to make a press release more readable on a screen.

News releases today often contain links to multimedia—audio and visual elements (photos, videos, graphics) that can add appeal to a news release and foster online engagement. However, when writing a release, carefully choose links that will add value; irrelevant links will only irritate readers. Think about including a call to action in the body, or what you want your reader to do as a result of reading the news release. For example, do you want your reader to go to a website? Download an article? Sign up for a newsletter? Buy tickets today?

A newer element being used in news releases is the *hashtag*, a label preceded by the symbol # that marks keywords in a topic. If, for example, the news release is about an event an organization is sponsoring, say a race sponsored by Nike and Warner Bros, the hashtag might read #LooneyTunesRace.

The length of the news release varies tremendously. Some experts say to keep news releases to one screen to avoid making the reader scroll down. Others say keep releases between 500 and 800 words. A good rule of thumb is to make the news release as long as it needs to be and not one word longer.

Quotation. News releases almost always contain a quotation from someone highly placed in the organization. These quotations generally appear in paragraph two or three of the release and are simply additional details or facts coming from an authoritative individual. In practice, quotations are often contrived by the author rather than obtained from the speaker. The quote never repeats information that appears elsewhere in the release, nor should it contain "fluff"—meaningless words that will be a turn-off to a busy journalist or blogger. In fact, PR Newswire suggests writing quotations that make a key point in 100 characters so that they can be tweeted.[3] Quotations should sound conversational and should not use hackneyed words such as "excited" or "incredible."

Follow these rules when using quotations:

- Use the exact spelling and title of the quoted person (called the *attribution*).

- Include the first and last name the first time a person is named and the last name thereafter.
- Put commas and periods inside quotes.
- Attribute each quote.
- Introduce each person quoted. (Example: Mark Elliot, recipient of this year's award, said, "I am grateful for the opportunity to serve my community.")
- Use "said" rather than "laughed," "snorted," and the like in news releases.

Contact. All news releases also contain information about who to contact for more information and how to reach that person. Include both e-mail and phone number. That information may appear at the top of the release, as the final sentence, or appear in both places.

Boilerplate. The final paragraph of most news releases is the "boilerplate," a short summary of about 50 to 100 words that provides background information about an organization. It may include what the company produces, the number of employees or outlets it has, its stock-trading information, or its corporate philosophy. It is common to set the boilerplate apart from the body of the news release with the subhead "About Company XYZ."

Figure 3.2 illustrates a template for standard news releases.

Style, Tone, and Objectivity

News releases must never appear to be advertising—no media outlet wants to give free publicity! This means that the writing voice and tone should be objective rather than persuasive. As you compose a news release, think about a skeptical, cranky editor, blogger, or customer having to wade through obvious fluff. Your words will be wasted on such individuals.

The following pointers on style and tone will help your news release achieve its purpose.

- Keep word choice neutral and accurate. Avoid overblown adjectives and instead rely on strong nouns and verbs to make your point. Be factual, clear, and succinct.

COMPANY LOGO

PRESS RELEASE

Contact:
Name(s)
Company
Phone (day and evening)
E-mail

Headline Written in Upper and Lower Case Boldface and Centered

Subhead written as sentence and italicized

CITY, State—Month Day, Year—After an "m" dash, begin the first paragraph. Write one to three sentences maximum per paragraph.

Single space with double space between paragraphs unless a specific traditional media source requires double spacing.

"Remember that quotations should be meaningful, link to the lead, and sound conversational," said Important Person at Name of Organization. "Place punctuation inside of quotation marks and avoid overblown adjectives such as *awesome* or *incredible*."

Feel free to use bulleted points for ease of reading if the content lends itself, thus:

- You may add links to images or other media for readers.
- You may include social media share sites.
- It is understood that the date of the release and the dateline are one and the same.
- If printed, the news release pages must be numbered at the bottom of page one (Page 1 of 2) and on the top of the second and subsequent pages (Page 2 of 2).

About Name of Company Issuing Release (Boilerplate)

The boilerplate should provide enough information for the reader to understand the organization's mission. Always end a boilerplate with the organization's URL and the phrase, "For more information, visit www.companyname.com"

# # #
(these symbols signify the end of the release)

Figure 3.2 News release template

- Be correct. People in the media consider themselves writers, so news releases must be well written and tightly edited. Typos, misspellings, grammatical errors, or incorrect format will turn off readers. Follow a style guide such as *The AP Stylebook*.
- Decide if the release is hard news or more of a feature news story. News releases can be written in either a hard- or soft-news style. Hard news is timely and has immediacy. Soft news focuses on people or issues that affect people's lives. A soft news release (a *feature*) might take the form of a story about a child whose life was saved by a new drug, with the issuing company being the drug manufacturer.

See the Appendix for an example of a news release. The following link leads to an excellent example of a news release issued by Bank of America: http://newsroom.bankofamerica.com/press-releases/community/worlds-top-professional-wheelchair-athletes-compete-fall-2015-chicago-new-y

Feature News Releases

Feature news releases differ from traditional news releases. They are not necessarily based on a timely event such as a new hire or product and do not use the terse summary lead.

Feature news releases are appropriate when an organization wants to publicize a product or service using an angle. For example, if you work for a potato grower, you might want to send a feature release about new recipes, especially as a tie-in to a holiday such as Thanksgiving. If your organization manufactures prosthetic legs, you might issue a release about a patient who won a marathon running on your product. The media are always interested in human-interest stories.

Features also highlight consumer news. For example, a utility company might issue a feature release, "10 Ways to Cut Your Gas Bill." A pharmaceutical company might send a release "How to Avoid Catching the Flu." Whatever the angle, always include the following elements when writing a feature news release.

Headline (mandatory) and subhead (optional). Feature headlines need to be catchy and forecast the main idea ("Put Some Bite into Teeth Cleaning") to better your chances an editor, reporter, or blogger will take a second look at your release. A subhead, as in a hard news release, is optional and should follow the same guidelines.

Delayed lead. Feature releases use a delayed lead instead of a summary lead. Instead of summarizing the news values in one sometimes-lengthy sentence, a delayed lead uses a captivating hook to lure your reader to continue reading. It should be no more than a sentence or two and should end with a clear statement of the release's main idea. This statement is similar to a traditional feature story's "nut graf" (short for *paragraph*), so called because it contains the essence or main point of a feature "in a nutshell."

The following is an example of a delayed lead with a nut graf.

Martha Bledsoe was one of hundreds who crossed the finish line at the recent Viceroy 500 Half Marathon. But what made Martha different was that she's 73.

[Nut graf] Seniors like Martha are part of a growing trend of elderly participants in athletic events once reserved for the young. But while these golden agers may be young at heart, their hearts aren't so young. And that means the active elderly must be extra careful when training.

The actual story will go on to discuss how the active elderly must exercise care when training for a strenuous athletic event. The organization issuing the story would be promoting its product (perhaps a knee brace or special running shoes) in a subtle way.

Body. Unlike a hard news release, the body of a feature is not written in an inverted pyramid style. Instead, feature releases have an internal organizing element such as steps or events that occur over time. When composing a feature release, use quotations from a variety of sources, and follow the same quotation guidelines noted earlier. If the release provides URLs or phone numbers that consumers can use for more information, place these at the end of a paragraph in case an editor wants to omit them to save space.

Clever ending. The end of the feature release will also differ from the hard news release. Rather than the boilerplate, end the feature news release by returning to the catchy beginning. If you opened by describing a runner with a prosthetic leg pushing through the finish line, end by returning to that arresting image. Sum up the essence of the story by reminding the reader of the main points. Or end your feature release with a helpful URL or another source for more information.

Using the previous example, we might end the release like this.

Martha says she plans to compete in a triathlon next year—with her twin sister. "It might be the first time in 70 years that I beat her!"

A good feature example can be found at http://www.prnewswire.com/news-releases/your-childs-next-homework-assignment-just-might-be-play-more-video-games-300124418.html

Submitting News Releases

As we have discussed, many organizations today simply upload their news releases to their websites under specific tabs labeled "News" or "Press Room." These releases are posted in date order with the most recent news release appearing first.

However, if you are sending a release to a media outlet, check to see if the publication has particular parameters to follow. The Los Angeles Times, for example, has very specific guidelines about how and where to submit a news release. Many online services exist that will submit your news release for you, but these are fee-driven and do not come cheap. The best way to get your news picked up by both traditional and new media is to have a great story to tell that will appeal to a large number of people.

Conclusion

News releases have been labeled the workhorse of the PR professional. Although their role has changed as the media adapts to technological innovations, the news release continues to be a key ingredient in any public relations mix.

News release checklist

News release item	✓
Complete contact information included: name, phone, e-mail address	
Headline is objective, tightly written, newsworthy; omits articles	
Subhead, if used, does not repeat news in headline; adds another layer of information and is written in a complete sentence	
Lead includes news values and main point of release	
Body is in inverted pyramid style, with more important news higher in story and details of news lower in story	
Quotations are not fluff but actual news put into the mouth of an appropriate company official. Quotations follow guidelines and punctuation rules	
Boilerplate contains enough information to adequately identify company scope, mission, and size	
Submission is formatted correctly. Company logo (optional) appears at top with one space above and below headline. Body copy is single spaced with double-spacing between paragraphs	

CHAPTER 4

Newsletters

Newsletters—regularly issued mini magazines or newspapers—are an effective way to build relationships with a group's stakeholders. Whether geared to supporters of a nonprofit, employees of an organization, members of a community, or any group with a shared concern, newsletters report on news or matters of interest in a succinct style. Ranging in length from a brief notice of upcoming events to a dozen or more articles, newsletters are comprised of regular topics called standing items and one-time, stand-alone pieces. The newsletter is often a significant component of an organization's communications and outreach. Once produced solely for print audiences, the newsletter genre is thriving in the digital world. The large number of online newsletter template offerings is one indication of how popular this genre continues to be.

From the reader's perspective, newsletters can be eagerly anticipated or a waste of time, depending on the way they are written and the type of content they include. But because they can help members of a group feel included and informed, newsletters are an important tool in the PR writer's arsenal—when done correctly.

Types of Newsletters

Newsletters fit into several categories:

Employee newsletters, also referred to as "house organs," are one of the most common types written. Formatted like a mini newspaper, these newsletters are intended to foster goodwill among diverse workers. Employee newsletters offer news about the organization and notices of policy changes, and they feature stories that highlight the accomplishments of a department or an individual. An employee newsletter might include an interview with the CEO or report on a new product or an award received. Employee newsletters are valuable because they make staff members feel valued and part of a team.

Member newsletters are sent to people who have joined a group. These common newsletters feature articles of interest to people who either support the organization currently (e.g., a paying member) or were part of a group at one time (e.g., alumni of a university). Clubs, professional organizations, and other groups use newsletters to keep members informed about events and opportunities for involvement. They are also a way to reach out to new members by illustrating what the group is doing.

Community newsletters are distributed to those who live in a specific area and who share concerns about their neighborhood.[1] These newsletters provide information about the quality of life in the area. For example, the local water district may send out a quarterly or biannual newsletter to all residents to update them on water quality issues.

Special-interest newsletters are designed to appeal to people who share a hobby, an interest, a perspective on an issue, or a trade. Sometimes special-interest newsletters are available by paid subscription only, so relevant content is especially critical.

Newsletter Audience Analysis

Before designing the content for any newsletter, start by defining its audience. Are the potential readers employees? Paying members of an organization? Everyone living in a geographic area? Subscribers? Refer to the "Audience Profile" (Table 1.1) in Chapter 1 to chart the specifics about your readers.

Be sure to assess the audience's diversity and its knowledge about the topic. For employee and member newsletters, the audience may know a good deal about the organization. However, depending on the organization's size, the audience may vary by gender, age, position held, and duration with the group. For community newsletters, the writer will need to take into consideration the various cultural differences and education levels of the readership. All these particulars should be considered when selecting newsletter article content and writing style.

People who subscribe to newsletters expect valuable information on a specific topic. For example, the *Kiplinger Letter* forecasts business and economic trends and is read by a wide swath of business professionals. The *Mayo Clinic Health Letter* contains articles on medical and health issues geared to a lay audience. Countless newsletters address a topic of shared interest such as the goings on at a retirement home or a preschool. Whoever your readership, you will need to know as much as possible about the readers' knowledge of your group or topic to create an effective newsletter.

Newsletter Purpose and Frequency

Once you have determined the newsletter's readership, think about what you want the newsletter to accomplish. Is your purpose to urge members of your group to become more involved? Do you want to keep readers updated about your organization's accomplishments? Are you sharing a new way to work on a hobby? Whatever your goal, a newsletter's function does not change with each issue, so it's important to be clear about your strategic purpose before designing the newsletter.

That being said, most newsletters are informative. Sometimes the purpose of that information is to simply add to the reader's knowledge. Other newsletters will use information as a way to encourage people to buy a product or service. Whichever is the case, writing to inform is different in style and tone than writing to persuade. We'll discuss the way to write articles for newsletters next, but it's important to remember that a newsletter's content needs to be worth spending time on. Articles cannot be perceived by your audience as filler or fluff.

Newsletters publish regularly, whether that is weekly, monthly, or quarterly. Since putting together a newsletter requires time and therefore a financial commitment, be realistic about how often you can produce a newsletter that will be eagerly anticipated. Then stick to the schedule.

Print Versus Online: Pros and Cons

As we have discussed, newsletters can be effective public relations tools. They have the potential to influence a huge number of people, thus increasing the organization's reach. It is common to see both print and electronically published newsletters, each having its benefits and drawbacks.

Hard Copy Newsletters

Hard copy newsletters continue to be used for several reasons. For one, many people enjoy receiving subscription publications in the mail. Because hard copy newsletters are printed on sturdy paper, they have almost the same staying power as a magazine and can be kept for future reference. Print newsletters are not always mailed; they can be distributed at various pick-up locations where members and nonmembers alike can have access to them. And of course, print newsletters are essential if your readership does not have convenient Internet access.

The primary negative of print newsletters is the expense. Paper, printing, and mailing all add up to a hefty bill (and are not eco-friendly), and if the newsletter is published frequently, those costs can be prohibitive. Secondary negatives exist as well. If mailed, print newsletters take longer to receive than electronically delivered ones. Keeping addresses up to date can be time-consuming. And finally, print newsletters require camera-ready layouts. Whether a staff member has the knowledge to use a newsletter template or a graphic designer has to be hired, the print newsletter must be delivered to the printer ready to be printed.

Electronically Distributed Newsletters

Distributing a newsletter electronically has both pluses and minuses. Electronically distributed newsletters are fairly inexpensive to produce, although the amount of time writing and keeping addresses updated is not insignificant. However, be aware of the downsides to electronically distributed newsletters.

Most online newsletters arrive via e-mail, and we all know that people delete e-mails without giving them a second thought. Spam filters may automatically remove your newsletter from a recipient's inbox. Even if the reader bothers to open the e-mail, click-through rates vary. When I wrote an e-newsletter for a commerce website, we were thrilled when an article had a 16 percent click-through rate. Yet despite these negatives, there is every indication that online newsletters have become a regular part of online content.

Electronically distributed newsletters take several forms. Some are delivered to an e-mail inbox in HTML (i.e., web page style). These newsletters can fill one or two screens with headlines and short summaries of articles called *blurbs* or *decks*. Links with the full story take the reader out of the e-mail and to a stable web space.

The HTML newsletter in Figure 4.1 uses a typical page format from which the reader can access a variety of specific articles. The article headline is a link, and the short descriptive line below the headline—the blurb or deck—provides a summary of the article's main point. The newsletter's timely content makes it valuable to its readership.

Figure 4.1 The University of California Santa Barbara HTML newsletter

Source: Reproduced with permission. © 2015 The Regents of the University of California.

Another type of e-newsletter is a plaintext version. Plaintext newsletters are sent to an e-mail address and usually include links to a series of articles that the reader can scroll down to peruse. Although they do not contain the visuals found in digitally produced HTML newsletters, plaintext newsletters are often sent in conjunction with an HTML version of the same document. There are several reasons that it's important to think about having both plaintext and HTML versions of a newsletter. First, plaintext newsletters pass through SPAM filters. Second, some people prefer reading plaintext e-mails on their mobile devices, which often cannot open the HTML version. For example, the Apple Watch can only open a plaintext newsletter.[2]

Some e-newsletters are considered e-zines and are essentially a short magazine-style website. Oftentimes subscribers to these newsletters are made aware of a new issue via an e-mail notification. Old issues are generally archived on the site so that readers can refer to them. E-zines are read the same way as a website and can therefore include as many of the bells and whistles available with HTML as the publishers deem necessary.

Research and Writing Newsletters

Determining your newsletter's content is a big job. You'll want to keep a file on your desktop with possible article ideas you come across between issues. But whether you are writing news briefs about upcoming events, summaries of events that already occurred, or updates about policies or opportunities, you will need to conduct research before you write.

Some newsletter material is gathered using traditional research methods. Comb the media (print and online) for current events, news, research, or other relevant and timely information that your readers would find interesting. Subscribe to newsletters yourself to make sure you know what others are writing about. Sometimes, however, newsletter writers must collect information from a primary source by conducting interviews. Learning how to interview and be a good reporter is an important element in creating your newsletter.

Interviewing

Many newsletter articles require the writer to conduct interviews to gather the information necessary to write. Interviewing can be broken down into three parts: before, during, and after the interview.

Before interviewing someone, set up a convenient time and place for the meeting. Do as much research on the situation or person before your meeting so that you appear well prepared. Come armed with a list of questions you believe your readership will expect you to ask. Devise shorthand for words you know you'll use during the interview so that you can take notes quickly. Dress appropriately for your interview, and show up on time.

During the interview, be sure to develop a rapport with your subject. Be friendly but professional. You may tape an interview only if the interviewee gives you permission. However, understand that some people may not be as forthcoming if they see a recorder. Always be prepared to take notes quickly and accurately. Some people use their computers or tablets to take notes. When using a laptop or tablet, be sure to continually make eye contact with your subject. Don't worry about correct spelling, but do be sure you have plenty of battery power. Always have a backup to your computer—a notepad!

Begin an interview with easy questions: correct spelling of the name, length of time with the organization, title, and the like. Don't interject your opinions; your job is to elicit information from the interviewee. Use a good mix of open- and close-ended questions. Open-ended questions leave subjects free to digress or give opinions. A typical open-ended question would be, "What do you like best about your position?" A close-ended question elicits a very brief answer. Asking someone, "Do you like being president of the club?" can only produce a yes or no answer. Your objective is to gather as much information as possible so that you have material that will allow you to write the most vibrant article possible.

If you will be asking difficult questions, wait until after you have gathered answers to your other questions. It is possible the interview will take a less pleasant turn after delicate questions have been posed or that the interview will even end, so never begin with an uncomfortable question. Preface the question with, "I know our readers will want to know ...."

At the end of every interview, ask if you may contact your interviewee later in case you have questions. You generally have one shot at a backup call, so gather all your questions beforehand.

After the interview, transcribe your notes immediately while the meeting is still fresh in your mind. The sooner you fill in holes, the better. Finally, you may want to send a thank-you note, and let the person know when the newsletter article will run. Refer to the Interview Checklist that appears at the end of this chapter.

Writing Newsletter Articles

Newsletters combine standing and one-time items. *Standing items* are recurring articles, similar to a column in a newspaper. A standing item for a newsletter might be a president's letter, an employee-of-the-month feature, or a spotlight on a department. *Sporadic items* are one-time articles that deal with news that will occur only once. For example, a house organ may have a one-time article about the company picnic or a new employee benefit. A member newsletter might feature a one-time article reporting on the results of an annual marketing survey.

Newsletter articles can be broken into three basic styles: inverted pyramid, feature articles, and news briefs. Both news and feature-newsletter articles tend to be short—about 300 words. News briefs are one to two sentences.

The *inverted pyramid article*, which we covered in our discussion of news releases in Chapter 3, mimics a typical news story reporting on an event that is about to occur or has happened in the immediate past. Referred to as "hard news," these types of articles require a serious or objective tone. Articles appearing in subject-specific subscription newsletters use this style almost exclusively.

Inverted pyramid articles begin with a *summary lead* that answers the basic news values of who, what, where, when, and why or how. The summary lead is the article's first paragraph and contains the gist of the entire story. The lead sentence is often long, up to 35 words. The remainder of an inverted pyramid article consists of facts written in descending order of importance that explain the main idea voiced in the lead. These facts are written in paragraphs of two to three sentences. Keep sentences on the short side; aim for 20 words or so.

The best way to tackle writing an inverted pyramid article is to first write down all the facts, one per line. You will have a list of sentences. Then home in on the main point that can be phrased in 25 to 35 words as the lead. One way of finding the lead is to look for a quotation that backs up the main point. Next, go through the remaining facts. Number them in importance as they pertain to illuminating the main point. The last point should be the least important fact. Inverted pyramid stories do not have formal endings; they just end with another fact.

Inverted pyramid stories attribute information to a source. Information coming from inanimate sources such as studies, organizations, or databases is attributed with the phrase "according to." Information coming from people is attributed using "says" or "said" and may be paraphrased or directly quoted. Using direct quotes gives articles objectivity because the information is being reported in the words of the individual quoted. Each time a new person is quoted, a new paragraph is used. (See Chapter 3 on "News Releases" for more guidelines on using quotations.)

To attain objectivity, inverted pyramid stories should avoid a writer's voice. Objectivity is achieved by using words that are not loaded or that show opinion. ("Sadly, crafters who rely on this method will be woefully disappointed.") Inverted pyramid stories should also be wary of using the second-person construction (using "you")—this usually means the author has not found the appropriate noun. Speaking directly to the reader may be appropriate in some articles, but inverted pyramid stories do not fall into this category.

Feature articles are stories that go beyond the facts of news and often put a human face on an event or organization. They may take the form of a Q&A, a behind-the-scenes look at a business or an event, a how-to, or a testimony. In newsletters, many features are profiles of members or leaders of the organization. Features differ in tone and style from inverted pyramid articles; they are lighter and brighter and can have a slant or angle. Using narrative techniques, features often supplement our understanding of an event or organization by showing how it affects people.

Features begin with a *delayed lead* that entices the reader with a hook. In a few sentences, the lead uses a *double entendre*, an unexpected question, or a catchy anecdote that epitomizes the main point. Some features begin with a scene setter, or a description that leads us to the main point. For example, if the feature is about an individual, the writer may lead with a description of that person's workplace:

> *Walk by Marsha Brook's cubicle and you can't help but notice the walls covered in souvenirs. From the plush Peruvian llama atop her file cabinet to the photograph of a dog sled race in Alaska, Marsha's distinctive workspace looks like a travel agent's instead of a market analyst's.*
>
> *That's because when Marsha isn't collecting data at XYZ Inc., the veteran traveler is working toward her goal of visiting every country in the western hemisphere.*

Notice the chatty style of the lead. This style more than anything distinguishes features from news stories. In features, second-person address—that is, talking directly to your reader—is common, as is the conversational tone and style.

The second paragraph in the previous example is called the nut or *nut graf* because it contains the article's *focus* in a nutshell. When using a delayed lead (as compared to a summary lead), the article's main point must appear close to the beginning of the story or the reader will become confused. Features don't ramble or simply report facts in a linear fashion. They tell a story with a beginning, a middle (the body), and an end. The nut graf should be the story's angle, or the approach the writer has taken to report the information contained in the story.

If the lead of a feature hooks the reader with a cute or catchy description or anecdote, the body contains the details that explain and amplify the lead. Similar to making points in an essay, the body of a feature is a narrative that is organized in a logical way. In features, *quotations* are sprinkled throughout to drive home a point. As narratives, features also use description or "color" to draw a picture in words. Features use anecdotes—short stories that illustrate a point—as a way to explain a key point or to add life to a story. Finally, features often contain background information a reader may need to fully understand the story's impact.

A feature has a formal conclusion called a *kicker*. Simply put, a kicker returns to the lead to complete a story's circle. In our previous example of Marsha Brook, our kicker might return to a photograph or the cubicle:

Come August, don't be surprised if you see a new piece of memorabilia on Marsha's cubicle wall. She's off to Uruguay next week.

The kicker concludes the story and gives the reader a sense of completion.

Feature stories in newsletters may encompass an array of topics. They may be "how-to" articles, lists of 5 or 10 points (e.g. *Ten Ways to Avoid the Flu*), profiles of members or leaders, or summaries of events told in an entertaining style. They may be heartwarming or humorous, although humor is a difficult style to pull off well—what is funny to you may be offensive to a reader, so be sure to think hard about how your words may be taken by your audience before trying humor.

News briefs are usually one-paragraph descriptions of events, products, or other items. They summarize main points in a tightly written, well-constructed, easy-to-read blurb. Some newsletters feature many news briefs on one page. The important point to remember when writing news briefs is to be concise; eliminate every extra word but be sure to include all necessary information.

Writing Headlines

All articles must have a headline. Good headlines grab a reader's attention but do so in a way that doesn't mislead or confuse. Some tips for writing headlines follow:

- Include the article's main idea.
- Use strong nouns and verbs in active rather than passive voice.
- Avoid "to be" verbs if possible.
- Write in truncated language that omits articles and prepositions.
- Have fun with feature headlines but do so in a way that still conveys the article's main point.
- Read your headline aloud to hear its rhythm and to make sure it flows.
- Create interest by using colorful, powerful language.

Some articles also include a subhead, or a *deck head*. Deck heads come after a headline, are often italicized, and are written in a complete sentence that builds on the information in the headline. Deck heads never repeat the news contained in the headline.

Images and Cutlines

All newsletters that go beyond text-only format should include art, that is, images such as photographs, charts, and the like. Readers' eyes immediately go to any visual. They will look at the image, read the caption, and then if interested, go on to read the article. Avoid clip art if at all possible and instead use photographs. Be sure to get permission to use photography; it is illegal to download most images from the web without permission or paying a fee.

Captions or *cutlines* do not point out the obvious ("Garth Veyda smiles at coworker Arlene Goodwin.") but instead reflect what a photograph illustrates ("Manny Dodds from finance and Alisa Bales from marketing compete in the balloon-tossing contest at last week's company picnic."). Avoid using judgmental words that characterize a photograph ("horrendous" or "ecstatic") or assuming you know what an individual in a photograph thinks or feels ("Candelaria Lopez loves striking out her boss, Marcus Weil."). Always be sure you have spelled names correctly, and be concise.

Content Layout

To achieve the best readership levels for your newsletter, the placement of articles requires some strategic thinking. The following discussion will be helpful as you design your newsletter.

Print Newsletter Layout

A print newsletter should take space into consideration. Length of articles, where to place art, and size of headlines are all dictated by the amount of space. If designed as an 8½ × 11 in. mailer, half or one-third of a page must be allocated for the mailing address. The front page of a print newsletter must include a *banner* with the publication's name or logo, the volume and issue number, the publication date, and an index with a table of contents as is illustrated in Figure 4.2. The image at the top links to an article on the back page of the newsletter. The article beneath the image fits the allotted space.

It is a good idea to place two main stories and at least one photo or other image on page 1. This way you double your chances of enticing readers to pick up and read the newsletter. If the articles do not fit perfectly on the page, you may need to "jump" the remainder to an interior page.

The inside pages of the newsletter sometimes contains the *masthead*, which is a box with the names of the publisher, editor, and perhaps contributors. It may also include an address and other publishing information. The content of the articles on the inside pages is up to the editor's discretion. Inside stories may include a letter from the president or CEO, announcements, short news briefs, Q&As, or a spotlight feature on an

Figure 4.2 Front page of **The Lens**

individual. It is common to see pull quotes in a newsletter. Pull quotes are quotes taken from an article that epitomize a main point. They are usually boxed, bold-faced, and in a larger font size than the body copy.

Many print newsletters use the top half of the back page for mailing information: the sender's and recipient's addresses and postage. The space below the fold is often reserved for a calendar of the organization's upcoming events. If you choose to place an article on the back page, it should fit the space exactly. Avoid placing jumps from inside articles on the last page.

Electronic Newsletter Layout

An electronic newsletter's layout varies depending on which format is used. In text-only e-newsletters, a list of all articles generally appears at the top of the screen. Text-only newsletters require the reader to scroll down to read individual articles or to arrive at the live link that will take the reader to the entire article. Readers of text-only newsletters will only click through to articles of interest.

If your e-newsletter is in HTML, decide which stories are most likely to draw in readers and put those at the top. Remember to think of the audience's needs, not the organization's. You may want the reader to jump right to your special offer, but that is probably not the primary reason your reader is receiving and enjoying your newsletter.

If your newsletter is housed at a website, you'll want to have tabs across the top and links along the left side that take readers to regular, standing items. Readers don't like scrolling down, so keep articles short, around 300 to 400 words unless your topic demands more depth and space. Your home page should have an index of the articles in each issue, and in that index, you can add links to articles that do not fit into categories under your tabs.

Newsletter Design Basics

With the plethora of templates for both print and electronically produced newsletters, some writers might not give design much thought. However, all public relations written materials need to emphasize readability, and a document's appearance contributes to how it is read. The following is a broad overview of some design basics that can be applied to creating your newsletter.

Print Newsletter Graphic Design

Most print newsletters use the 8½ × 11 in. page layout because this common size is easily stored in a binder. This size can also be used in a horizontal or vertical format. The number of pages is determined by the budget and the amount of information that needs to be communicated. A short newsletter is four, 8½ × 11 in. pages, but the page count can increase by two- or four-page increments.

The 8½ × 11 in. page must be divided into columns. Avoid wide columns; try to keep character count to 45 for a two-column format and 36 for a three-column design. (A character is a space, punctuation mark, or a letter.) If you justify margins, use appropriately placed hyphens to break up words rather than the awkward spacing caused by keeping words whole. A ragged right column is not as tidy looking as a justified column, but it's easier to read than justified columns without hyphens.

Choose no more than two font styles; use a sans serif font such as **Calibri**, **Verdana**, **Arial**, or **Helvetica** for headlines because they have clean lines and stand out. For the body, take readability into consideration when you choose a font. Serif fonts such as **Cambria**, **Times**, or **Times New Roman** are easier to read because they form a line at the bottom of each letter that the eye can follow. When using a serif font, single-space your lines and double-space between paragraphs. Do not indent to indicate a new paragraph. However, if you use a sans serif font for the body of your newsletter, be sure you have enough leading (the space between lines) so that the copy is more readable. It is worth noting Word's newer default line spacing. Some prefer its more open appearance, but if you are at all conscious of space, you'll want to stick to single spacing.

It makes sense to unify your newsletter's look and feel with the rest of your PR materials, so make sure that the colors and fonts you choose work with, not against, your other printed pieces. Select a color scheme and stick to it, working with one or two complementary colors that blend with the shade of the paper. For example, you may choose royal blue boldface for headlines and a gold band of color going across an antique white page. Use black for body copy type and avoid colors that will be hard to see or that are hard on the eyes (yellow or fuchsia). If your budget allows, print your newsletter using the full spectrum of colors (called four-color). This will allow you to print color photographs, which adds liveliness to a publication.

Graphic devices—boldface, italics, underlining, boxes, shading, rules, and bullets—should be applied consistently and sparingly. Remember that graphics are symbols used to communicate visually. For example, *boldface* draws attention to words. A *rule* separates one item from another. *Italics* tell a reader that a word deserves special attention. A *shaded sidebar* next to a longer story links that information to the adjacent piece but separates it at the same time. *Bulleted points* list items so that the writer doesn't have to be repetitive. It's usually unnecessary to use two graphic devices on any one item; to boldface and underline a headline, for example, would be redundant.

Electronic Newsletter Graphic Design

Writing for the computer screen differs from writing for a printed page. When preparing your electronic newsletter, consider these tips:

- Keep line width to 60 to 70 characters maximum per line. Tracking more than 70 characters diminishes readability.
- If you justify margins, use hyphens to break up words rather than the awkward spacing caused by keeping words whole. A ragged right column is not as tidy looking as a justified column, but it's easier to read than justified columns without hyphens.
- Use a sans serif font like **Verdana**. These clean, modern fonts produce a clearer image on the screen than do serif fonts.
- Be aware of color use for background and font. White type against a black background should be used sparingly, not for entire pages of content. Avoid colors that will distract from the copy.
- Take advantage of space, and supplement your copy with images that add interest to your newsletter.

Your electronic newsletter's appearance is just as important as its content, so take some time to examine existing newsletters for ideas.

Conclusion

Newsletters remain one of the best ways to reach your constituency. While print versions are still used, easily uploaded online newsletters will continue to gain in popularity. Your ability to write and design a newsletter can only increase your value to an organization.

Interview checklist

Before the interview	√
Set up convenient time	
Conduct research, prepare questions	
Devise shorthand for faster note taking	
During the interview	
Dress appropriately	
Develop rapport with subject	
Tape only if given permission	
Take accurate notes	
Make good eye contact	
Bring backup note taking material if using technology that could break down	
Get correct spelling of source name	
Use mix of open- and closed-ended questions	
Obtain usable quotations	
End interview by asking if you can call with further questions if necessary	
After the interview	
Transcribe notes immediately	
Fill in holes	
Send thank-you note	

CHAPTER 5

Brochures

Brochures have a permanence that makes them important in public relations. Used to inform or to persuade, brochures provide readers with valuable information while conveying a sense of an organization's professionalism and stability. Brochures proliferate in every walk of life, from large and small organizations to nonprofits to educational institutions to politics and government. Considered a staple of public relations communications, brochures are used to make an organization and its offerings known in an attractive, informative document. Most brochures are printed, although some organizations make brochures available electronically. Although these e-versions of brochures are less expensive to produce compared to printing, they put the onus of printing them out on the consumer and lack the professionalism that comes from presenting a slick, attractive hard copy.

Brochure Audience Analysis

Many brochures are aimed at an external audience that has either requested or seeks more information about a product, service, task, or an organization. A couple may request a brochure about a time-share; a small business owner may examine a brochure about a bookkeeping service; a homeowner may pick up a brochure that describes how to lay tile. In large organizations, brochures may be produced for an in-house audience to provide information about benefits, procedures, or opportunities.

Whatever the case, writers must start with a clear picture of the brochure's end user. Is the potential reader a new mother who needs information about when to vaccinate her baby or a possible client wishing to examine the qualifications of a consultant? Either way, the writer must be acutely aware of the reader's English proficiency and knowledge of the topic. When sitting down to create a brochure, the first step must be to develop a thorough audience profile.

Often a brochure is part of a major promotional program. In that case, the organization has likely invested in surveys that produce detailed information about the consumers and their attitudes, including a demographic and psychographic profile. This information is crucial for the writer to produce the kind of copy that will push the consumer to react to the product or service offering. With or without a survey, writing effective brochures requires a thorough understanding of the target customer's needs and wants, and its copy must appeal to those distinct requirements. If you have to, conduct your own small survey. You may also want to consult the *Local Market Audience Analyst* published by SRDS, which provides buyer profiles.

Refer to the information in Chapter 1 to prepare an in-depth audience analysis before proceeding to write your brochure.

Brochure Purpose

A brochure's purpose must also be clarified before beginning to write. Is its goal to lure high-end buyers to a new housing development's groundbreaking event? Does the brochure need to explain an official's ideas to constituents? Or must it provide the nuts and bolts about a club or organization?

When thinking about the purpose of a brochure, it is helpful to understand that brochures fall into two main categories.

Informational brochures describe a procedure (such as how to install a tile backsplash) or provide information about an organization, a condition, or a topic (e.g., an "Education Abroad Program at a University" or "How to Cope With Depression"). These types of brochures are practical and efficient.

Persuasive brochures are written with the objective of selling a product, service, or idea. Because they are produced by the company selling the product, persuasive brochures highlight only the best points about whatever is being sold. Still, persuasive brochures work best when information is presented in objective language without sounding "salesy."

When writing a persuasive brochure, the writer must know where it fits into the promotional mix or selling cycle to decide on the type of information to include and what writing style to employ. A stand-alone piece, for example, must contain all the information the reader needs to complete the desired action. A brochure that is part of a series may need to repeat certain information that appears in all the brochures. How a brochure is used will fall into one of several stages of the buying process.

An **inquiry response** brochure is written to provide more information in response to another promotion, such as a television commercial or a print ad. These brochures provide many details about whatever is being marketed and are aimed at someone who has already shown interest. Inquiry response brochures include information about how to purchase whatever is for sale.

Point of purchase brochures are placed adjacent to an item that requires detailed information about its use. For example, a brochure showing the steps necessary to apply decorative paint might be placed near a store's display of paint products.

Sales support brochures are compiled to provide sales staff with comprehensive information about the product or service. They can be used during a sales pitch to illustrate a product's features or benefits. Other times, sales support brochures are called "leave behinds" because a salesperson will leave the brochure at the end of a sales call to act as a reminder about the product or service.

Writing Brochure Content

The first step to writing your copy is to conduct research. You must know your product inside and out before you can write one word about it. Good writers begin this process by immersing themselves in the product, service, or organization. Visit a factory if you are writing about a product. If you are writing about a group, go to the organization and interview members. Watch how something is done until you understand enough about it so you can to explain the process clearly.

Gather all pre-existing written materials—ads, web copy, testimonials, press kits, and audiovisual materials. The writer must fully understand all aspects of a product or service, the way that product or service is viewed in the marketplace, how the competition measures up, and the strengths and weakness of the product or the service. Without this background information, creating an effective brochure will be impossible.

Successful brochures integrate the *features* and *benefits* of whatever is being promoted. Features are the physical characteristics of an item (or the activities and mission of an organization). A benefit is how a feature adds value to a product. For example, some pens have retractable nibs. The benefit of that feature is that it prevents ink from leaking. A feature of membership to an art museum is that members may view exhibits before they open to the general public. The benefit is that members do not have to stand in line or fight crowds to view exhibits.

A helpful way to understand the difference between features and benefits is to create a features and benefits table. Doing so provides you with concise words and phrases to use to write copy. Table 5.1 is a sample features and benefits table for Headphonies, a three-inch portable speaker that plugs into tablets or smartphones.

Table 5.1 *Features and benefits of Headphonies*

Features	Benefits
Small, compact, lightweight	Carry it anywhere
Cute, trendy designs	Choose your design to match your personality
$24.95 price	Affordable and less expensive than alternate speakers

The next part of research involves conducting a thorough analysis of the strengths, weaknesses, opportunities, and threats involved. This is known as a SWOT analysis. Strengths and weaknesses are internal, that is, inherent to the product or service. Opportunities and threats are external and are beyond the control of the manufacturer or organization.

Let's say you are writing a brochure for a travel destination, New Orleans, intended to promote a specific tour, product, or event. You need to know what draws people to the city and what affects their decision to visit. This requires knowing all the features and benefits of travel to New Orleans as well as its strengths and weaknesses as a destination. It is wise to create a SWOT analysis for your product whether it is a location, a bar of soap, a service, or a group. Table 5.2 is an example of an abbreviated SWOT analysis of New Orleans as a destination.

Table 5.2 SWOT analysis of New Orleans as a destination

Strengths	Weaknesses
Unique architecture and charm, world-class restaurants Varied hotel options Fun, party atmosphere with many events (Mardi Gras, Jazz Festival)	Perceived danger and criminal activity Reputation of corrupt officials Some tourist attractions perceived as unsanitary
Opportunities	**Threats**
French Quarter charm Abundant home, garden, and food reality shows may attract visitors	Hurricane season could deter visitors from planning visits

From the SWOT analysis, you as the writer would build an even more specific list of points to be aware of when creating the brochure copy. For example, if research has shown that potential visitors are worried about criminal activity or unsanitary conditions, you would need to note that the city is functioning better than ever since its comeback from Hurricane Katrina. If we know potential visitors are interested in food and architecture, it makes sense to feature photographs of unique Cajun and Creole dining options in the picturesque, quaint French Quarter.

The final step before writing brochure copy is to complete a *project brief*, a document that defines the goals and parameters of a copywriting task. One of the most important elements in the project brief is the idea of a primary message. A *primary message* is the one main point that must be conveyed. It is the heart and soul of a brochure.

To market a Southern Hemisphere beach destination to Americans during the U.S. winter, the primary message might be "When it's winter in the United States, it's summer in Brazil." The copywriter bolsters that main idea with *key support points*. These are features and benefits of travel to the destination as defined in Table 5.1 and the SWOT analysis (Table 5.2). A template for a project brief appears at the end of this chapter.

The second step of creating a brochure is to write the copy. Copywriting for a brochure differs from writing news releases or newsletters.

First of all, brochure images are as important as the prose, so the copy must work in tandem with the visuals. Second, some brochure writing (such as that for glitzy sales pieces) requires copywriting skills adopted from advertising. On the other hand, informational brochures work best when they do not use overly flowery prose or exaggerated claims to make a point. You must be aware of these stylistic differences when writing a brochure.

Brochure Writing Style

Writing a successful brochure requires a distinct writing style characterized by finesse and profound control of words. While some brochures are used to inform, ultimately they must persuade the reader to act in some fashion. As a writer, you will need to be aware of these tools and strategies before tackling brochure copywriting.

Conciseness

Brochure writing uses a strategy called *chunking*. Chunking arranges information into bite-sized portions with headings and subheadings, short paragraphs, and short, easy-to-follow sentences. Since space is at a premium when writing brochures, copy must be tightly edited to omit all unnecessary words and redundancies. Use the strategies for omitting wordiness described in Chapter 1 when you write and edit your brochure.

Conversational Tone

A brochure often uses a casual style to inform and persuade. The prose should flow naturally, as it does in a conversation. As we have discussed, the best way to attain fluid prose is to read the copy aloud so that you can hear and edit sentences that begin the same way, are choppy, or are lengthy and hard to follow. Work toward a mix of long-, short-, and medium-length sentences that avoid jargon. Rely on hardworking nouns and verbs that communicate more directly than flowery adjectives and adverbs. Feel free to begin sentences with conjunctions such as "and" or "but."

Parallelism and Bullet Points

Parallelism is a writing strategy used by all good copywriters. Parallelism means matching nouns with nouns, verbs with verbs, phrases with phrases, and questions with questions. Readers expect parallelism, especially in sets of two or three items. Using parallel phrasing sets up expectation in the reader and, when used correctly, delivers a punch the reader will appreciate.

Often, brochures use a list to supply information succinctly. When doing so, writers frequently organize the material into bulleted points. When listing items, always use parallel structure. If you are using a verb to begin the first point, use a verb for every point. The same goes for a noun or a phrase.

Positive Voice

Brochure copywriters use positive words to make a point. Instead of saying "New Orleans is no longer dangerous" a copywriter would emphasize the positive and say, "Enjoy nonstop fun in America's most vital and unique city." An accompanying photo might show a couple strolling at night on Bourbon Street or a family posing with a policeman in front of Saint Louis Cathedral. Avoid negative words or phrases that can convey an unfavorable connotation and rephrase in a positive way. Instead of "No discounts will be honored after May 1," say "Discounts will be honored through April 30."

Use of "You"

Using the second person is a good way to achieve a conversational tone when writing a brochure. When using "you," remember the writer is speaking directly to the reader, so save this technique for appropriate topics and audiences.

Organization

Brochures are not read in a linear fashion. People will focus on bold face headings and visuals before they begin to read the copy. And even then they will not read the copy in a linear fashion, that is, starting at the beginning and reading through to the end. Even so, the copy must be organized logically, which means the brochure must be written in a linear fashion; we cannot just haphazardly lay down information. There must be a natural flow of ideas.

When organizing a brochure, sort information logically so that readers can easily locate points. Begin by creating an outline from which you can write headings and subheadings. Under these, jot down how you will explain or deliver on the promise of the heading. Since you won't know how many pages the brochure will be until you have completed the copy, write your copy before laying out the design. Aim for tightly edited prose to minimize cost; brochures should only be as long as they need to be. Be complete, but use as few words as possible. Make every word fight for its life.

Front Panel

The front *panel* (also referred to as a cover) must draw in the reader two ways: with a compelling visual that communicates as much about the brochure topic as possible and with a title or name that explains the topic. Say you are creating a brochure to encourage parents to vaccinate their children. The cover photo might include a happy mother and baby and a title such as "Protecting Your Baby: A New Mother's Guide to Vaccinations."

Figure 5.1 is the front panel of an informational trifold for a high school art program that features student artwork and the organization's name. Its artistic design emulates a portfolio review and invites readers to learn more about the program.

Many brochure covers also include a snappy slogan, also referred to as a *tag line*. Tag lines are a great way to emphasize the main selling point or advantage being illustrated. While tag lines come to be identified with a product or service in an organic way, they take lots of trial and error to create. If you decide to create a tag line, begin by jotting down everything you can think of that is beneficial about the organization, product, or service. Whittle down your list to five of the most important aspects, and then home in on the one you want to emphasize. From there, distill your

Figure 5.1 Front panel of trifold brochure

message into a pithy, memorable saying. Shorter is always better than longer!

Finally, resist the temptation to put too many words on the front panel of your brochure. Doing so is a turn-off to readers.

Inside Panels

The inside panels can be seen as one large page and can be divided vertically, horizontally, or a combination of both. If you are using more than eight panels, include an index so that the reader will know where to find specific information.

Begin the "story" of the brochure on the upper left inside front panel. (You may be tempted to introduce your topic on the right column, but that ignores the instinctual way English speakers approach reading—from left to right.) To introduce the brochure, you might describe the product or organization, highlighting customer benefits. Rather than listing features, the inside spread should emphasize how the product, service, or organization meets the needs and wants of the reader. Organize the information in the inside spread in the way your reader will likely respond best, but always remember to arrange your story in a logical fashion.

Say we are composing the informational brochure promoting vaccinations. The inside spread might be broken down into a series of logical questions that act as headings and that forecast the entire brochure's content:

- What are vaccines?
- Why does my baby need vaccines?
- Are vaccines safe?
- When should my baby get vaccines?
- How will my baby react to vaccines?
- Do vaccines have side effects?

Notice how the organization of the questions mirrors a story with a beginning, middle, and end. And from simply reading the headings, the reader understands the brochure's story line. The story may be "Three easy steps to choosing your next dishwasher" or "Ten facts you need to know when traveling abroad," but the answers tell a story to a reader who needs to know these answers. The brochure delivers information written in a clear, conversational style that is not overtly self-serving and that shows that the writer understands the readers' needs.

Figure 5.2 is the inside spread of an informational brochure and illustrates how to use columns and headings effectively.

The panel that the reader sees on the right when the brochure cover is opened is sometimes referred to as a "wild card" because it is considered separate from the inside spread. Here is where you might place testimonials, a teaser to encourage the reader to look inside, special offer, or forms and the like.

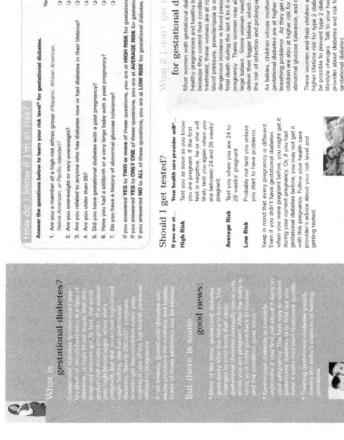

Answer the questions below to learn your risk level* for gestational diabetes.

	Yes	No
1. Are you a member of a high-risk ethnic group (*Hispanic, African American, Native American, or Pacific Islander*)?	○	○
2. Are you overweight or very overweight?	○	○
3. Are you related to anyone who has diabetes now or had diabetes in their lifetime?	○	○
4. Are you older than 25?	○	○
5. Did you have gestational diabetes with a past pregnancy?	○	○
6. Have you had a stillbirth or a very large baby with a past pregnancy?	○	○
7. Do you have a history of abnormal glucose tolerance?	○	○

If you answered **YES** to **TWO or more** of these questions, you are at **HIGH RISK** for gestational diabetes.
If you answered **YES** to **ONLY ONE** of these questions, you are at **AVERAGE RISK** for gestational diabetes.
If you answered **NO** to **ALL** of these questions, you are at **LOW RISK** for gestational diabetes.

Should I get tested?

If you are at...	Your health care provider will*...
High Risk	Test you as soon as you know you are pregnant. If the first test is negative, he or she will likely test you again when you are between 24 and 28 weeks' pregnant.
Average Risk	Test you when you are 24 to 28 weeks' pregnant.
Low Risk	Probably not test you unless you start to have problems.

Keep in mind that every pregnancy is different. Even if you didn't have gestational diabetes when you were pregnant before, you might get it during your current pregnancy. Or, if you had gestational diabetes before, you may not get it with this pregnancy. Follow your health care provider's advice about your risk level and getting tested.

What if I don't get treated for gestational diabetes?

Most women with gestational diabetes have healthy pregnancies and healthy babies because they control their condition. Without treatment, these women are at risk for: high blood pressure, preeclampsia (a sudden, dangerous increase in blood pressure), and fetal death during the last 4 to 8 weeks of pregnancy. These women may also have very large babies. Some women need surgery to deliver their bigger babies, which can increase the risk of infection and prolong recovery time.

As babies, children whose mothers had gestational diabetes are at higher risk for breathing problems. As they get older, these children are also at higher risk for obesity, abnormal glucose tolerance, and diabetes.

These women and their children also have a higher lifetime risk for type 2 diabetes. It may be possible to prevent type 2 diabetes through lifestyle changes. Talk to your health care provider about diabetes and risk from gestational diabetes.

What is gestational diabetes?

Gestational diabetes is a kind of diabetes that affects women only. It is a type of diabetes, a high blood sugar, that only pregnant women get. In fact, the word gestational means pregnant. If a woman who had high blood sugar while she was pregnant, but she better (had high blood sugar before) she has gestational diabetes. Nearly 200,000 pregnant women get this condition every year, making it one of the top health concerns related to pregnancy.

If not treated, gestational diabetes can cause problems for mothers and babies. Some of these problems can be serious.

But there is some good news:

- Most of the time, gestational diabetes goes away after the baby is born. The changes in your body that cause gestational diabetes normally occur only when you are pregnant. After the baby is born, your body goes back to normal and the condition goes away.

- Gestational diabetes is treatable. If you find out about it early in your pregnancy. The best way to control gestational diabetes is to find out you have it early and start treatment quickly.

- Treating gestational diabetes greatly lowers the baby's chance of having problems.

Figure 5.2 Inside brochure pages

Back Panel

Readers often ignore the back of a brochure, so it should not contain any critical information. The backs of many brochures simply list the firm's contact information and logo. If the brochure is being used to sell, make sure the back includes all the information the customer needs to carry out the next step in the buying process. Using the earlier New Orleans example, the back cover might tell the reader, "Contact your travel agent or call us at 123-456-7890 to book your trip today!" If the brochure is being mailed, the back panel may be used for the address and postage.

Headings and Subheadings

The headings and subheadings tell the brochure's story. A reader should be able to understand the gist of the content from examining heads and subheads. But boring heads can be counterproductive. Try to be reader-oriented when writing headings; think about which reader benefit you can emphasize rather than which point you can illustrate. For example, instead of "About MarketPros," say "How MarketPros Delivers." Use words that pack a punch.

Try to write parallel headings. If you are using questions, use them throughout. If you begin each heading with a gerund, the *ing* form of a verb used as a noun (e.g., "Choosing Your Baby's Doctor" and "Watering Your Orchid"), make all the headings gerunds.

Subheadings are subordinate to the heading under which they fall. If you use subheads, make sure the reader understands they are related to the heading and that all subheads mirror each other graphically. Like the boxes on an organizational chart, heads and subheads should have equivalent weights. This can be achieved with a graphic device such as a color, font, or shading.

Visuals

Brochures marry words with images to create meaning and to stimulate action. Visuals in a brochure must be powerful rather than extraneous and are used to illustrate a key point related to the primary message.

Knowing when and which visual to use is a specialized skill. For this reason, many firms employ a graphic designer to lay out brochures.

Sometimes existing visuals must be used. In that case, the writer must work around whatever is available. Remember that it is illegal to download copyrighted images. Your company may be sued or fined if illegal use of an image is discovered.

Matching Visuals to Content

The type of visual used depends on what is being communicated. In general, brochures contain photographs, charts or graphs, diagrams, illustrations, and maps.

Photographs should be used to show a product in action. Imagine a brochure about a car without an image of that car driving on the road. Sometimes a firm will hire a photographer to shoot a product so that it is professionally lit, or even go on location to shoot the product. A good photograph is as important to a successful brochure as a good copy.

Some brochures use *illustrations, diagrams, or drawings* in lieu of photographs. For example, if you are writing a brochure about atherosclerosis, a gory photograph of a clogged artery would be difficult to look at; an illustration better communicates the concept. In some cases, a diagram or illustration must be used. No photograph can illustrate the food pyramid, for example.

Charts and graphs are the clearest ways to illustrate data. *Bar charts* are used to compare items. For example, a bar chart could be used to differentiate between the increase of male and female smokers over a given time period or show year-end earnings from two divisions. *Pie charts* show parts of a whole. A pie chart is a good way to illustrate the components of an advertising budget or where membership monies are allocated. A *line chart* or graph shows changes over time. Perhaps you want to show how earnings have increased since 2000. A line chart helps the reader visualize this data. A *flow chart* illustrates a process or a procedure.

Maps are used to illustrate location. Most travelers will want to view the route of a tour; in this case, a map would be critical. If you want to illustrate a business's location, you might include a street map rather than written instructions. Remember to omit unnecessary information when using a map as an illustration. Show only what the reader needs to see.

Design and Layout Basics

Designing a brochure can be a highly creative endeavor requiring mastery of graphic design applications such as Photoshop, Adobe InDesign, and Adobe Illustrator. It can also be quite simple; an 8½ × 11 in. trifold can be designed in Microsoft Word and many word-processing applications. Whichever way you go, design the brochure *after* writing the copy.

The following are a few design basics to keep in mind as you write.

Color. Brochures can use one color (usually black and its permutations of gray), two colors (black and one other color), three colors (black and two other colors), or four colors, meaning the full color spectrum. Typically, brochures with color are more expensive than black-and-white brochures. But using a four-color format gives photographs depth and realism and provides designers with more choices. When using color, be aware that some colors are difficult to read. For example, try reading yellow type for any length of time! Stick to black or dark colors for most of your copy. If you want to use color for headings, make sure they are readable. And do not go overboard; pick a color scheme of two or three colors at the most.

Font. Type fonts are divided into two basic types: *serif* and *sans serif.* Serif fonts such as Cambria, Times, Garamond, and Book Antigua have "feet and tails" that create a line of sorts to help the eye track, which is why most novels, newspapers, and other material with dense words use serif fonts for copy. Sans serif fonts like Calibri, Helvetica, Arial, and Verdana do not have the feet and tails on serif fonts and feature a more modern, clean look to them. (Notice how the 12-point font appears different in each of the previous examples. This is because of something called the font "x-height," which is the height of a font's main body.)

Sans serif fonts create a clean line that makes them eye-catching for headings and more easily read on a computer screen. But reading lots of type in a sans serif font can tire the eyes. Many designers use sans serif fonts for headings and a serif font for body copy. Bear in mind that font styles connote meaning; **Comic Sans** is playful and fun, but no one would want to read an annual report written in it!

Odd shapes. A way to make a brochure stand out is to use an odd shape. A brochure for gardening tools in the shape of a trowel may encourage readers to pick up the brochure and buy a product. The problem is cost. An odd-shaped rather than standard-sized brochure requires die cutting, which is expensive to produce.

Placement of copy. When laying out a brochure, consider two page-design basics. One is the *Z pattern*. As stated earlier, because English is written from left to right, readers look at the upper, left-hand side of a page first and use a "Z" pattern to follow narrative. The points of the "Z" are natural spots upon which the eyes rest, so designers place less important text on those areas. The second is to view a page as a *grid*. Each page is a blank sheet that can be divided into various sections or grids. A four-page, 8½ × 11 in. brochure has an inside "blank" of 17 × 11 in., requiring several different grids or columns. Think of grids as ways to separate ideas you express in your copy. A grid can be differentiated with color, rules, lines, photographs, or other graphic devices.

Paper. Paper choice affects printing quality and price, so the type of paper a brochure is printed on matters. Thin paper will bleed color; heavy, glossy stock will be difficult to fold. Colored paper will affect photographs and readability. A good printer will know the pros and cons of various paper choices and can help you understand these distinctions early in the design process.

White space. Space without illustrations or copy is referred to as *white space*. Some designers lay out pages with a lot going on; others prefer clean lines with plenty of white space. While no formula exists for deciding on a good balance between clutter and white space, remember to keep messages visible and to think of how the reader will react to the visual design.

Conclusion

Brochures, because of their staying power, continue to play an important part of any firm or organization's promotional mix. From a simple photocopied trifold to an intricate 16-page splash on glossy stock, brochures illustrate a company's message and are often a consumer's only point of contact with an organization. Taking the time and effort to design a brochure that effectively meets readers' needs will result in an invaluable component of a company's public persona.

Project Brief Outline

Project name:

Project description: What needs to be produced? (1/2 page B&W ad; four-page, four-color brochure, etc.)

Background: Describe what research has been uncovered about the product, especially in relation to competition. Describe the competitive arena and any specific communication situations that may be encountered.

Primary message: What is the *single* primary message?

Primary benefit: What is the target audience's *single* primary benefit?

Key support points: What features and benefits will be used to support the primary message?

1.

2.

3.

4.

Tone: What overall tone should this project convey?

Publicity objectives: What marketing objectives are we trying to achieve?

Target audience: Who are the readers, viewers, and customers of this project? Describe any needs and perceptions they have about the product.

Current target audience perceptions: What is the audience's current attitude about what this project addresses?

Desired response: What do you want the target audience to do or think as a result of the project?

Mandatory elements: List specific images, logos, phone numbers, and so on that must be included in the project.

CHAPTER 6

Media Kits

Public relations (PR) professionals are routinely called on to put together media kits, a collection of materials providing facts about an organization, its leadership, its products, an event, or an issue. As the name denotes, media kits are intended for use by the media and should not be confused with packets designed for sales support. Although a kit put together for sales may contain many of the same elements as a media kit, its purpose is entirely different.

Media kits are used to supply the media with background about an organization or the necessary facts to cover an event. That event may be a news conference given by an organization explaining a product recall (such as the recent Takata airbag recall); it might be an introduction to a new product (think about Apple Watch); it might be a PR disaster (the Refugio oil spill in Santa Barbara). In all cases, the organization would provide a media kit containing salient information.

Traditional media kits are hard copy, but increasingly this is changing. Some organizations provide digital versions of a media kit (DMK) on their websites. The benefit of this approach is that information can be updated regularly, thereby making it more timely and less expensive than a print media kit. Still, the hard copy media kit continues to be a staple of the PR function.

Media Kit Audience

Media kits are put together to provide information to those in print, radio, television, or digital-based media. Editors and reporters form an uneasy alliance with PR practitioners; both need one another to exist, but both are skeptical of the other's motives. Knowing this, the PR professional must serve the organization while not antagonizing or alienating the media. The contents of a media kit should be well written to appeal to a discerning audience and objective to appeal to this audience's sense of ethics.

Media Kit Purpose

Media kits are designed specifically to provide background material a reporter or news entity needs to cover an event or feature a subject in an article or radio or television broadcast. Therefore, this material should be complete, well written, factual, and objective. Nothing will make a reporter less inclined to write a good story than a self-serving media kit.

Typically media kits address distinct purposes:

- News conferences: events to provide reporters limited access to a celebrity or organization spokesperson
- Special events: sponsored event or program reporters have been invited to
- Promotions: introduction to new products, exhibits, or tours
- Crises: incidents that require regular updating for reporters

The contents for these types of media kits vary and will be discussed next.

Media Kit Appearance and Contents

The materials for a print media kit are placed into an attractive one- or two-pocket folder. An image of the product being promoted or the company's logo is often affixed to the cover. The stock quality, cover image choice, and printing of these folders all work to create an image. A folder with a glossy, four-color photograph and metallic touches connotes a glitzy event or product, whereas a folder made of high-quality stock with matte finish and embossed with a company logo produces a more conservative image. Folders vary vastly in price, but if kept simple they can be relatively inexpensive to produce. For digital media kits, a link on the organization's website or a separate tab will guide the reader to various links that include the materials for the specific media kit.

Often organizations print a large number of folders to have on hand for various purposes. Sometimes the folder is designed to be multifunctional.

Other times, an organization may create a separate folder for a specific event. In both cases, this shell for the contents is the first thing the media sees and should be created with the tastes and needs of the media in mind. All folders should include a die cut in which a contact person's business card is placed.

The contents of media kits vary, but all tend to include the following:

- **Fact sheets**: A tersely written overview, the fact sheet should be on letterhead and comprise boldfaced headings and bulleted points. It may include an overview of the organization with names of principals, number of employees, address, location(s), contact information, and the like. A fact sheet may be about a new product with product specifications; it may provide the facts of an upcoming event or a history of an event, the organization, or milestones. It will answer the standard news questions: who, what, where, when, and why. These items should be organized in the inverted pyramid (most important information first).
- **News releases**: A specially prepared news release about the event or subject may be accompanied by previous pertinent news releases.
- **Bios**: A one-page description of each of the organization's main players accompanied by a headshot of reproducible quality. Bios can be straightforward and simply discuss the executive's experience and accomplishments at the organization, or they can be narrative and include more personal details.[1]
- **Nonprint items**: If broadcasters are covering the event, they will require video. Visuals should be included in the media kit and be written with the media's needs in mind. Only offer high-quality images and video.
- **Backgrounder**: The backgrounder provides an explanation of the mission, history, and strategic vision of an organization written in paragraph style with an objective tone. This document can go into depth about the organization, even explaining day-to-day operations.

Optional items or those items that would only be included for a specific event include the following:

- **White paper or position paper**: A *white paper* is a technical report that educates readers about an issue or a topic. A *position paper* is opinion based and conveys an organization's stand on an issue.
- **Past news articles**: Any time an organization has had press coverage, the organization has tear sheets of those articles reproduced. These are often included in a media kit to illustrate that the organization has been worthy of media coverage.
- **Spokesperson's statement**: A spokesperson's statement is a quote or quotes from an individual speaking on behalf of the company or organization designated to go on the record. These include the spokesperson's contact information.
- **Pitch letter**: Pitch letters are persuasive letters to an editor or writer of a specific media vehicle proposing an idea for a story. (This is discussed in more detail later in the chapter.)
- **Cover letter**: Addressed to a specific journalist, the letter will name the kit's contents, a rationale for covering the event, and contacts for more information or interviews.[2]

The organization and placement of the items in a media kit should be logical and easy to follow. If there are many pieces, a list of included items similar to a table of contents could be used. In addition, the media might find it helpful to have all the materials reproduced on a flash drive, which should also be placed in the folder.

The contents of the different types of media kits are illustrated in Table 6.1.

When I worked at a software firm, we had a media kit area in our offices. In it were dozens of printed pieces in separate slots. These pieces included various news releases, reprints of articles about the firm and its leadership, product information sheets, brochures, director bios, and more. These sheets were available to the staff for both sales and marketing purposes. It was a popular spot!

Table 6.1 Media kit contents

Media kit type	Content
News conference	Basic fact sheet on organization; news release with quote of high-placed individual; backgrounder on specific individual, if appropriate; visuals to complement story
Special event	Basic fact sheet on organization; fact sheet on event, including its significance and all particulars; historical fact sheet; story ideas or actual feature articles; visuals; contact information for interviews or more information
Promotion	Basic fact sheet on organization; specific fact sheet on event and product; bios of principals; reprints of news stories and(or) reviews on event and product; visuals to complement promotion; story ideas for journalists; contact with name and contact information of source that journalists can interview
Crisis	Basic fact sheet on organization; backgrounder on organization; bios of principals; historical fact sheet; statement from high-placed person in organization about response to crisis; contacts for press to interview; regular updates on situation; visuals for print and digital media; links to other sources

Pitch Letters

A pitch letter is crafted to capture the interest of the most jaded of readers: an editor or reporter. Pitch letters are used by organizations to prod an editor or reporter to cover a story featuring the organization's product, service, or event. For example, a foreign country might hire a U.S. PR firm to raise awareness of its nation. As part of the overall PR strategy, the PR representative might write a letter to a travel magazine writer or editor hoping that the idea pitched in the letter would stimulate interest in writing about the destination.

If it sounds impossible, it's not … but it *is* difficult! Good pitch letters contain an angle that will appeal to both the editor *and* the readership or viewing audience. A successful pitch requires not just thinking the way the media thinks but also understanding that media's needs.

Pitch letters work best when the PR professional analyzes the publication (or other media) to understand the type of stories that are typically covered. Back issues or shows should be read or viewed to make sure the idea has not been done previously. Target a writer or producer who specializes in covering stories related to the idea being pitched. The better the background research, the better the chance the idea will be picked up.

A good pitch letter is tightly written and error free and includes the following elements:[3]

- Name of specific individual to whom the idea is being pitched.
- A professional tone. Don't become effusive or imagine that you are the writer's pal. That will just irritate a journalist.
- A first paragraph that reads as if it were the lead of the article; it should hook the reader with its captivating, feature article style.
- A second paragraph that describes how and why the story will appeal to the readers or viewers of the particular media, illustrating an understanding of both the publication or show and the reader or the viewer.
- A third paragraph that provides the terms of the offer: Is the story an exclusive? If so, for how long will you hold it? Discuss how you can help with setting up interviews or obtaining original art. Do *not* offer to write the story!
- The date by which you'll need to have a definitive answer. Be polite and thank the addressee.
- A sign-off with a simple "Sincerely."

See the Appendix for a sample of how a PR writer might pitch an idea to a journalist.

Conclusion

Media kits continue to be indispensable in PR. Whether they are distributed via a website or handed out at an event, media kits are versatile tools that help an organization promote its message. As with all writing for PR, media kits require the writer to be acutely aware of the audience's needs while simultaneously serving the organization's purpose.

CHAPTER 7

Website Content

A website has become as important as a company logo. Often offering the first impression to a member or customer, a website that is professional, easy to navigate, well designed, and clearly written is a basic business necessity that often falls on the public relations department to write. This chapter will focus on the attributes of successful websites, site organization, and typical content. But first, let's examine how reading on a screen differs from reading on a printed page.

Unique Characteristics of Web Writing

Beyond the rules that govern any good writing, web writing demands particular attention to clarity, coherence, and correctness. Web writers must become meticulous copy editors for typos, misspellings, or other easily fixed flaws because web readers are especially turned off by amateurish errors. In fact, studies have shown that such obvious inattention to detail gives a web source low credibility.[1] However, writing for the web is unique in some important ways.

- *Web writing is interactive*, unlike print writing, which is static. When we write for an audience that can (and likely will) give instant feedback, we need to remember to be respectful, polite, honest, and factual.
- *Web writing uses links* to take the reader to different levels of information, either within a site or to another site entirely. This means the writer must compose in layers, which affects both the organization and amount of information we write. It also means that we must write in bite-sized chunks of no

more than 100 words (called *chunking*) that form short paragraphs.

- *Web writing integrates words with other media.* We must
  think about what content we will highlight visually with
  photographs, charts, or maps and how audio or video might
  enhance our words.
- *Web writing relies heavily on design factors.* As web writers, we
  also must factor *design* into what we compose. In the past,
  the writer composed on a page with little thought about
  how it would appear to the reader. A layout artist took the
  manuscript or copy and created a final project. But when
  writing for the web, we must consider how our words will
  appear to our reader throughout our process. From font
  choice to the number of characters across a page to the length
  of paragraphs to color, design is the key to web readability
  and therefore becomes a major factor in how we compose.
- *Web writers know that readers have differing reading experiences.* Web composers must be aware that readers will have
  differing reading experiences depending on which browser they
  use, the quality of their screen, and the device on which they
  read (desktop, laptop, tablet, or smartphone). These variances
  require a heightened sensitivity to making our prose clear as
  well as other strategies we'll discuss later.
- *Web writers are not automatically seen as experts.* Web readers
  do not automatically consider web writers as experts, unlike
  print authors. Print authors have been published because
  of their authority or knowledge and have adhered to
  agreed-upon standards by those in a position to publish the
  work. But anyone can author web text, so web content writers
  cannot automatically assume readers will trust them. Web
  writers earn the trust of their following by being transparent.
  Sometimes this actually means admitting to a bias. We'll talk
  more about voice and how and when to use it, but for now
  remember that just because you write it does not mean you
  will be taken at your word.

Web Reader Habits and the Writer

Researchers have learned that reading on the web is quite different from reading a printed page. As we have discussed, when English readers read a printed page, they start on the upper left corner and continue reading in a "Z" pattern. Thus, readers of print typically begin where the author intended and continue reading until the end. This pattern is called linear.

All that changes when reading on a screen. Web usability guru Jakob Nielsen has famously explained how people read on the web by saying "They don't."[2] Web users scan. They skim. They scroll. They peruse. But they do not begin at the beginning and keep going until the end. They scan impatiently because they are looking for something, and they want to find it fast.

Web usability experts have also determined that users read web pages in an F-shaped pattern: two horizontal swipes followed by a vertical swipe. The eye begins at the upper left corner of a page and then takes two quick horizontal glances followed by a vertical swipe down the left side.[3] This information is important because we need to place our words in locations we know the reader will intuitively look for them.

We also know that reading on a screen takes nearly 25 percent longer than reading a printed page.[4] One of the reasons for this is because screen definition varies greatly. Letters that are not crisp and clear are harder to read. And although new technology like retinal display is helping to improve screen definition, readers still must work harder to read on the screen.

Through research, we have learned that web readers spend 80 percent of their time above the page fold, a term taken from journalism that refers to the articles on the top half of a broadsheet newspaper. On the screen, above the fold refers to the area of the web page that is visible when first landing at the site. Although users do scroll, they allocate only 20 percent of their attention below the fold.[5]

Finally, web readers expect *visual logic* and *organization*, not just textual logic. They expect to seamlessly access information, so web writers must organize their content in layers and become conversant in the usability standards that enhance readers' web experiences.

The implications of web reading habits are huge for writers and impact everything from word choice, to sentence length, to the volume of what we produce.

Website Audience Analysis

The success of a website depends on how well the author can focus on a specific audience's needs and expectations, so first and foremost, be clear about those you expect to visit your website and why you want them to come. If you are marketing a product or service, you may be writing to current and potential customers because you want to sell something. If you are providing information, you may have to orient your reader, who may not know a lot about the topic or may be seeking advice. If a website's purpose is to provide a forum for your opinion on a topic, you may want to attract like-minded individuals or those interested in your subject.

Once you can concretely describe the type of reader you expect, begin to narrow your focus on some particulars. Through research, be certain about your intended readers' ability to understand written English and their facility with using the web. A detailed demographic and psychographic analysis will help you better understand your reader. Committing specific, research-driving data to a formal process will give you the information you need to best reach your audience. Whether you are targeting baby boomers, generation X, or millennials, you would want to use cultural references each group would find relevant.

Consider the elements listed in Table 7.1 when analyzing your website audience.

Table 7.1 Demographic–psychographic profile elements

Demographic information	Psychographic information
Age	Lifestyle choices
Gender	Values
Ethnicity	Attitudes
Income	Interests
Education	Needs–wants

Once you have defined these elements, you are better equipped to decide on the site's content and the style in which to write it. The style or tone of your website should appeal to your defined audience and its expectations. For example, a small business owner putting together a website has the freedom to choose how to appeal to an audience—the style may even have a "personality." Say you have a business that caters to young teenage girls. You may wish to convey a perky or cutesy tone with your web content. Perhaps you want to publish your views about a topic to an audience that is more blasé; you may want to adopt a "snarky" attitude. The mock political news site *The Onion* has a distinctly sarcastic tone. The entertainment site *E! Online* is gossipy. Whether a site's audience expects an attitude or an objective voice, the writer must deliver.

Many experts suggest creating a *persona* before writing web copy. *Personas* are fictionalized characters who represent a targeted market segment for a website and give the writer a more concrete person to address when writing the web content. Table 7.2 contains the elements you may consider when putting together a persona.

Table 7.2 Persona template

Items to include	Content explanation
Name	Create a name that is typical for your reader and that embodies an actual fictionalized reader
Photo	Include a photograph of your typical reader
Occupation	Describe your reader's work life
Web habits	Explain your reader's relationship to reading on the web
Quotes	Include quotations that come from actual interviews of potential readers or create several sentences that describe your reader's relationship to your product or organization
Knowledge level (specific to product or organization)	List your reader's perceptions and knowledge about your product or organization
Needs–wants (specific to product or organization)	Describe what your reader needs from visiting your site and how that differs from what the reader wants
Narrative	Create a narrative for your typical reader that illustrates his or her values, dreams, limitations, or other psychographic information

Websites for Large Audiences

If your site must convey professionalism, credibility, and trust, your tone and voice should reflect those values. Websites for large audiences—often written for huge organizations, educational institutions, or government agencies—generally use a voice decided upon at the corporate level. And although many authors may participate in producing this type of content, the writing voice must be unified.

Whatever tone or style the corporate voice takes, the audience for such sites will be very broad. You could be addressing anyone from current and future staff to stockholders, vendors, the press, and the general public. Traditionally, the writing style used by large organizations has been paternalistic: We are the experts; you (the readers) are the novices. This autocratic tone dominated all forms of business communication for many years and is still pervasive. However, writing for the web is moving further from this lecture-like style and more toward a tone that engages the reader by using more of a "we are all in this together" sensibility.

To help move large audience web copy toward this style, you'll want to use the "you" attitude, a style in which the reader's needs are foremost. The "you" attitude, unlike the more traditional business voice, assumes the reader is intelligent. (Have you ever gone to a doctor's office, been talked down to, and left thinking you either missed something or are just stupid? That doctor did *not* use the "you" attitude!)

Here are a few examples illustrating the "you" attitude.

Not using "you"	*Our services provide hundreds of needy children with ...*
Using "you"	*Your donation allows us to ...*
Not using "you"	*We require a verification on any check over ...*
Using "you"	*To protect you from fraud, please provide verification on any check over ...*

Website Organization or Navigation

Whatever the size of the company, all websites must provide recognizable organizational cues called *navigation* to guide readers to the information or other material they seek. Just as a reader of a print newspaper or magazine can quickly turn to specific content—the crossword puzzle, astrological forecast, movie reviews, breaking news—your website readers must be able to go where they want and understand where they are. Therefore, when developing web copy, it's important to have a clear picture of the site's organization.

A *site map* is a graphic depiction of a website showing hierarchical relationships between pages. Before writing your site copy, create this map and define the routes your readers will have to take to arrive at specific information pages. Site maps serve another function as well; they provide the information a search engine needs to locate your pages. Google provides a free site map generator available at: www.xml-sitemaps.com/

Part of creating the site map will require you to decide on navigation cues. Many sites contain *tabs* on the top of a page. For example, Figure 7.1 shows the home page for the National Institutes of Health (NIH). The tabs across the top of the page separate sections of information: Health Information, Grants & Funding, News & Events, and so on.

Figure 7.1 Example of clear navigation tabs

Websites, especially large ones, tend to have further breakdowns of categories beyond the tabs on the home page. These are often found along the left side, bottom, or other locations on a page. Larger websites use *pathway or gateway pages*, which are intermediary pages that guide readers to specific information pages. This type of page can be likened to a table of contents[6] and often comprises specific headings containing links to information pages. Large organizations whose websites contain many layers of information frequently use this approach. Figure 7.2 is a pathway page from the NIH home page shown earlier.

Figure 7.2 Pathway page with links

Orientation is another organizational element you'll want to consider. Notice how the example of the NIH page tells readers they are looking at a page called "Grants & Funding." By labeling the page with a clear title, you help your readers know where they are to better orient them.

Using the described strategies will help you create a well-organized site, a key to its success.

Types of Web Pages

As any web user knows, websites all have a home page and links to other pages. We will now discuss specific types of pages and the strategies to building effective content for them.

The *home page* is a website's "face" and should immediately express the site's purpose and set its tone or personality with colors, graphics, writing style, and visual markers. Readers don't spend much time on a home page, so its material should be organized intuitively, allowing visitors to quickly access information or begin tasks.

Home pages have five functions:[7]

1. Identify the site and provide graphic branding.
2. Set the site's tone and voice.
3. Help readers understand the site's purpose.
4. Allow readers to begin tasks.
5. Move readers to specific information efficiently.

Websites are often part of an integrated marketing and public relations effort and should reflect the same look and feel of whatever other materials the organization uses. The logo, color scheme, and artwork that are part of your organization's image should also be part of your website's *brand* and should be apparent on the home page.

Another function of home pages is to instantly let your reader know what the site is about. The home page for Business Expert Press leaves little to the imagination about the site's content. Likewise, the home page allows the visitor to immediately begin tasks in a streamlined manner:

You can also see that the Business Expert Press home page provides links to destination or information pages. These links should move your readers easily, intuitively, and efficiently to the information they seek.

Some sites have home pages that are exclusively visual. While these images can set a mood (such as a romantic photograph of a wedding or a hopped-up muscle car), I find them irritating. They require extra time and effort from the reader. A visual with no narrative forces the reader to think about where to click. It holds up information retrieval or beginning a task. Unless your readers will truly be lured by an eloquent image, use words *with* images on your home page.

Information pages are the meat of your website. They are characterized by the use of headings, subheadings, visuals, and links. Sometimes a link is accompanied by a "blurb," an abbreviated description of the content found at that link. Often the blurb is the first sentence of an article that is found in its entirety at the link. The following is an example of a link with a blurb:

Malibu's Hottest Rentals Live like a Hollywood star in one of our exclusive vacation rental homes.

Another characteristic of information pages is their organization. The narrative on information pages is frequently written in the inverted pyramid style, a staple of journalism in which the most important information appears at the beginning and lesser important facts follow, a style we have discussed earlier.

Individual web pages also organize material in the inverted pyramid style. When writing information pages, begin with the most important information to your reader summarized in the first paragraph. Arrange subsequent information in descending order of importance. Since readers may not scroll down, keep critical information to one screen and be aware that only readers who are very interested in a topic will stick with it long enough to scroll down several panels.

Remember to always, always, always trim your words. Edit ruthlessly! A basic rule to follow is to halve what would be written for print.[8] As you compose your information pages, remember the strategy of *chunking*. Chunking arranges information into bite-sized portions of about 100 words so that they can fit on one computer screen without requiring scrolling. Chunking is typified by abridged paragraphs and short, easy-to-follow sentences.

Another technique for writing effective informational web pages is to make text scannable. The following example illustrates a chunk of text on an information page that uses some of the techniques we have discussed.

Create Reader-Friendly Web Pages

We know reading on a screen takes about 25 percent longer than reading on a printed page. To make your web pages more reader-friendly, use the techniques below to improve text scannability:

- Headings
- Lists
- Short paragraphs (no longer than six lines)
- Boldfacing
- Lines confined to 60 to 70 characters

Remember to use easy-to-recognize words and to keep sentences under 20 words. Paragraphs should also avoid appearing too dense on the screen.

Website readers expect to see illustrations that support words. Can you imagine shopping online for clothing or shoes without seeing photographs showing different colors or styles? Would you plan a vacation without seeing images of the destination and accommodations? When you write, think about which images would communicate to your reader, and make sure the photographs you choose have high resolution to be sharp on the screen. But also make sure that the pictures communicate without requiring explanation. Remember that if a photograph is so small that we cannot read or see it, it's useless. Also consider your audience when choosing photographs. It makes good sense to choose photographs of your expected reader. Are they all women? All men? Diverse nationalities? You'll help your readers feel they are in the right place by showing them visuals in which they are represented.

Visitors to websites may also expect *multimedia* integrated into their experience: sound, video, and animation. When composing websites, think about how words can mix with visuals or sound to enhance meaning or provide another way of looking at information. An excellent example of integrating multimedia into content can be seen on the website for any newspaper. Visit *The New York Times* website on any day. Articles often have corresponding videos of the author discussing the story or a photograph gallery to accompany an article. It's worth noting that too much media interspersed within text can detract from meaning. Graphics and sound should be inserted to enhance meaning, not simply because it's technologically possible to do so.

Typical Website Content Pages

Although not all websites contain typical pages, the following ones are common enough to merit a more detailed discussion.

About: *About* pages are found on almost every reliable website. They provide a website with validity and authority. The *About* page is your chance to explain who you are, what you do, and why and for whom you do it. Organizations often include their mission or vision statements on the *About* page(s). A tab entitled *About* may also have various secondary pages with bios of key leadership, the organization's history, press releases, or position papers.

Contact: A page that includes the various ways a customer or another stakeholder may contact people within your organization is vital to any legitimate website. In many cases, these contact numbers or e-mail addresses go to an anonymous source, but some organizations list the names and direct contact information of key individuals. Depending upon the needs of your organization's particular situation, your site may also require instructions about how to return merchandise or other pertinent information, which often contains a link to e-mail and phone numbers for customer care.

Pressroom or Newsroom: Organizations routinely write news releases and post them on their websites. Posting news on your website serves several functions. News releases allow an organization to inform the public about its news, anything from announcing a new CEO or product to recalling a defective machine part. By posting a news release, you also provide the media with ideas for writing about your organization.

The Press page or tab serves another function. It can provide links to articles written by the media in which the organization is mentioned. A separate page for the press can provide vital information for the media typically found in a media kit. For example, the Santa Barbara Botanical Garden's website Press Room page has a link called "Media Assets" that contains images for the media to download.

Conclusion

Writing website copy requires understanding the unique needs of web audiences. Because web readers demand quick access to information, the writer must be especially sensitive to clarity and conciseness as well as providing clear navigational cues. Writing an effective website requires acute attention to an organization's or individual's purpose for visiting and using the site. The unique nature of the web as a mixed media vehicle provides writers with almost endless possibilities to embed other media within their words. In today's hyper-connected world, websites are a basic business necessity, and composing website copy is a requisite skill for every writer.

CHAPTER 8

Social Media

The world of social media has added another layer to the public relations mix. With the proliferation of social networking and video-sharing sites, blogs, and chat rooms, the web is crawling with online commercial communication. Successful organizations have caught on to the enormous potential these new media platforms provide and are making social media a vital part of their public relations strategy. In fact, the two-way conversation that lies at the heart of social media has become integral to an organization's presence.

Of course, writing for social media contexts requires skill and careful, consistent management. This chapter will focus on the most common types of writing found in social media: blogs, microblogs, and social networking sites. Before we begin, however, let us discuss how and why social media works.

Today's online audiences have come to expect that their opinions and voices will be heard and acknowledged. No longer willing to absorb an organization's message passively, online audiences demand that an organization engage with them. Part of that engagement is conducted via the organization's social media presence on social networking sites such as Facebook and LinkedIn, where consumers can post their reactions, comments, or opinions, and in blogs and microblogs designed to garner large followings to promote a brand or awareness.

Large enterprises and small businesses alike have jumped on the social media bandwagon. Intel, a leader in social media use, has an extensive online presence that encourages managers, vendors, and others in the organization who have completed social media training to engage with stakeholders. Intel has an entire division devoted to managing its online presence, which it uses to build brand loyalty.

Small businesses and groups have also adopted social media in increasing numbers. For those with limited public relations and advertising budgets, social media provides an excellent way to build a brand or increase a customer base. By connecting and engaging with stakeholders, small businesses, nonprofits, and other groups extend their reach in ways that were unheard of just a few years ago.

Social Media Audience Analysis

Social media has three main audiences: customers and clients, employees, and the media.

Customers and Clients

Current or potential customers and clients are the primary audience for social media. People interested in an organization, a product, an issue, or a person form the target audience for much of social media. These readers are a niche audience actively looking for information and for engagement.

To best reach an organization's current and potential customers or clients, the audience should be well defined. As with all writing tasks, writing for social media will be most effective if the content fits the needs and wants of the target audience. To create a more intimate and successful relationship with your social media audience, you should create one or several *personas* for these messages. A persona is a profile or an invented biography of a typical user or reader based on real audience analysis and data. For example, a university might create several personas as targets for social networking that could include newer alumni, older alumni, prospective students, and parents. Each persona has specific needs that could be targeted in various posts. (For an example of a persona template, see Table 7.2.)

It's also a good idea to monitor the activity of your competitors' social media to understand your audience. By watching the discourse between a competitor and its audience, you may gain important feedback that will influence your own communication.

Employees

Large organizations use social media internally to provide spaces for colleagues to share knowledge. These in-house channels of communication have become extremely useful ways to connect co-workers, especially in organizations with multiple locations. Internal social media is often unavailable to outsiders.

Media or Social Press

Public relations has always been about connecting with the media, but the definition of media has changed due to the influence of the 24/7 news cycle and the plethora of nonprofessional sources of information that proliferate on the Internet. Still, a primary role of the public relations practitioner is to engage with all forms of the media: traditional news media and journalists as well as bloggers and online reporters.

The traditional media—news editors and writers—comb the web in search of ideas for stories, interesting people, and news about organizations. Social media conversations provide the media with fodder for good copy, thereby allowing an organization to reach an otherwise fickle audience. And for unknown organizations, using free networking can be a way to attract the media's attention. By following a social media community's comments about a product or an organization, the traditional media can pick up on a new trend and write about it. In the eyes of the media, simply having an audience validates an organization or its product.

Bloggers are also looking for good stories from PR professionals. Just as with journalists, bloggers are hungry for the latest scoop. But unlike journalists, bloggers typically enter the conversation about an organization's performance or product. Today's public relations professionals develop relationships with bloggers just as they do with the traditional media.

Social Media Guidelines

Because social media encourages conversations with almost anyone, those conversations can devolve into a free for all with the potential to do a lot of damage to an organization. For this reason, many groups adopt social media guidelines. Intel was one of the first multinational organizations to do so and has made those guidelines available to the public.[1] The Intel guidelines can be found at www.intel.com/content/www/us/en/legal/intel-social-media-guidelines.html. They remain an excellent resource for any group that wants to create rules for its own social media presence.

Intel's "Social Media Guidelines" include three main principles: *disclose, protect,* and *use common sense.*

Disclose refers to being transparent and writing in the first person— Intel requires that anyone using social media on its behalf must identify himself or herself as an Intel employee. Furthermore, disclosure involves being upfront about having a vested interest in the topic. Lastly, disclosure includes talking to readers as if the conversation were face to face, using a friendly tone that avoids sounding pedantic. The final element of the disclose principle urges authors to write only about their area of expertise.

Protect means that no employee may violate confidentiality or legal guidelines. It serves to remind an organization's social media authors that writing online means writing on the record. This portion of the Intel's guidelines also bars slamming the competition and urges writers to be judicious about what they share.

Using common sense includes three points, the first of which is that social media must add value rather than take up space. This principle includes the idea that once authors have started an engagement, they must stay engaged—that is, not drop the ball. The final principle guiding Intel's social media use includes keeping a cool head and being careful and considerate. It also declares that mistakes should be admitted.

If your organization uses social media, you should create clear guidelines for all involved.

Social Media Formats

Simply put, social media are all forms of electronic communication between online communities who share various forms of content including information, ideas, messages, and visuals. In this section, we will discuss the most commonly used forms of social media.

Blogs and Microblogs

Blogs and microblogs work hand in hand. Often a microblog announces the presence of a blog, which contains the meat of the message.

Blogs—short for *web logs*—are actually websites with individual posts archived by date in reverse chronological order. Blog posts tend to be articles, reviews, white papers, or recommendations, but almost all have a bias or voice the author's opinion. But because blogs are so plentiful, they must contain relevant information that appeal to readers and invite an interactive experience. Therefore part of each message usually includes a link to video clips, photographs, other blogs, websites, or an invitation to post comments.

Blogs differ from a website in that they are dynamic and change frequently. Many blogs are the work of one author. However, it is not unusual for a blog to have multiple contributors, thus keeping the content voice fresh. News entities, corporations, government agencies, and individuals all produce blogs.

The media is a major player in the blogosphere. Established media like *The New York Times* and *Fortune* magazine, for example, have blogs whose content is written by a staff writer or a contributor with expertise on a topic. For example, a reporter who covers medicine for *The New York Times* may also contribute blog posts on medical-related topics. The articles differ from the blog posts, which are less formal, contain the writer's opinion, and offer a link to one or more sources. The news story published in the newspaper will be written in a more objective tone and may attribute a source but will not link directly to that source.

Organizations use blogs to communicate directly with consumers by offering useful, consistent, and interesting updates. Interactive blogs can be highly effective channels of communication that produce a lot of bang for a relatively low cost. When consumers sign up to follow a blog, for example, they may share that information with their own network of friends. By doing so, the number of people exposed to the information can expand exponentially. It is this massive sharing characteristic that makes blogs so popular with organizations.

Blogs frequently use Rich Site Summary (RSS) technology (also dubbed as *Really Simple Syndication*), which allows followers to keep track of a website. An RSS feed is a software application that aggregates syndicated content. When an author syndicates content, readers may sign up to follow those headlines, posts, or updates. Since a blog's goal is often to accrue followers who sign up to follow it, blog writers incorporate searchable words and terms into the copy.

Characteristics of Blog Writing. Blogs written for business, government, or nonprofit organizations can take many shapes. Most if not all are written using the inverted pyramid organizational style. They begin with a paragraph that summarizes the main point. All details supporting that point are then arranged in descending order of importance and contain the 5Ws and 1H of journalism: who, what, where, when, why, and how.

This example comes from a 360-word inverted pyramid post I wrote for *BizComBuzz*, a blog geared to college instructors who teach business communication.

New Research: Employers Want Smart and Socially-Savvy Workers

It's not enough for new hires to be smart or well educated. A new study indicates that employers also want their fledgling employees to have strong social skills.

Soon to be published in the Review of Economics and Statistics, the research drew connections between what employers say they want in an employee and high-paying jobs requiring complex interpersonal skills. Such abilities include problem solving, complicated communication required in directing and planning, and the vague "people skills" so frequently appearing in job descriptions.

The research, conducted by UC Santa Barbara professor Catherine Weinberger, showed that today's labor market demands higher-skilled workers who are not just smart but who are also well rounded. Only those who possess both skill sets reach the highest tiers of the corporate ladder.

Previous research has shown a direct correlation between non-cognitive skills demonstrated in high school and higher wage earning later in life, especially among high school athletes, leaders, and the socially adept. In the past, employers were content with hiring a worker who possessed either cognitive skills—i.e. book smarts—or social savvy.

The same is not true today. To assess the situation, Weinberger examined US government surveys from 1979 and 1999 that measured high school seniors' math scores and their earnings when they reached their late twenties. The surveys also contained data about students' social engagement in activities like yearbook, sports, or other outlets. Weinberger then measured skills required in different jobs. Some were managerial and required both social and cognitive skills. Others required one skill or the other, such as number crunching to measure cognitive ability or social adeptness needed in sales or marketing.

Weinberger's analysis showed that in today's labor market, both skill sets had to be present for the individual to earn more. In previous years, there was no additional benefit to having both sets of skills.

Her research also showed that students who are neither socially adept nor academically engaged are doing worse than expected and worse over previous years.

The ramifications for education policy are great, Weinberger says. The next questions to ask are whether people are naturally gifted in both areas or if they can be educated differently to give them stronger and more balanced bundles of skills as they enter the labor market, she adds.

Some blogs are written in a style that humanizes the dialogue between a company and its stakeholders. Consequently, the writing voice is more casual. In fact, some blogs read like a conversation with someone who has a distinctive voice. To capture that voice, using graphical elements (such as underlining, italics, or dashes) or turns of phrase that helps the blog *sound* like a conversation is not just allowed—it's expected. Look at the use of casual language in this paragraph from Lisa Eadicicico's post on *Business Insider*[2]:

There weren't many shocks at Google's annual developer conference, but the company did remind us of one area where it's blowing the competition away: teaching machines how to think.

Organizations use blogs to promote themselves or their brands. However, experts advise against the temptation to try to sell to readers or sound overly promotional.[3] Notices of sweepstakes, coupons, special offers, or contests should comprise no more than 10 percent of what the audience sees. Instead, the organization should focus on informative content, engaging conversation, links, and infographics.

Blog post content falls into several broad types, as follows:

- Narrative: tells a story or provides an analogy to engage readers while explaining a concept or complex process
- Interviews: transcribes or summarizes points from an interview with an expert on a topic
- Events: describes an event the organization participated in or hosted
- Informational: discusses a topic relevant to the audience

The screenshot in Figure 8.1 shows a post from one of the blogs published by the National Institutes of Health and is a good example of an informational blog post. You can read the entire post at http://blog.ninds.nih.gov/2015/04/24/how-stroke-prevention-promotes-healthy-brain-aging/#more-602

Figure 8.1 Information blog post

Before jumping in and writing a blog, spend some time observing the online community's conventions. Look for commonly used acronyms, jargon, and stylistic elements such as tone and language use. If you're going to become a member of a group, you don't want to stick out—you want to fit in.

Consider including the elements listed in Table 8.1 when you write a blog.

Table 8.1 *Characteristics of blogs for public relations*

Catchy, intriguing headlines—eight words or less is best
Keywords that contain blog's main idea; searchable words for Search Engine Optimization
Graphical devices such as *italics*, dashes (—), boldface, and punctuation marks (!) for emphasis or to emulate a real conversation
Length of 300–600 words written using inverted pyramid organization style
Bulleted points for readability and scannability
Short sentences that avoid long introductory phrases or dependent clauses
One-sentence paragraphs or very short paragraphs
Questions and invitations to reader to join the conversation
Blogrolls (links to blogs blogger recommends) or hyperlinks
Casual tone with relaxed adherence to conventional grammar (but no glaring errors that would poorly reflect on professionalism)
Tags, key word identification
Careful balance of information-share and self-promotion
Distinctive author voice, if appropriate
Artwork or some sort of graphic for visual interest

Microblogs

Microblogs are shorter than traditional blogs. They may be published using technologies other than the web-based methods, including text messaging, instant messaging, e-mail, or digital audio. Among the most notable microblog services are Twitter and Tumblr.

Microblogs help an organization create an online presence. Those who follow a Twitter account, for example, are interested in a particular subject, and therefore, anticipate tweets as a way of keeping posted and up to the minute. The way people follow topics is through a unique characteristic of microblogs called the *hashtag*, a word or phrase preceded by the # symbol that marks a topic by use of keywords. Hashtags make microblogs searchable and create the phenomenon known as *trending*. When a topic catches on and grabs the attention of many followers in a short time, that topic is said to be trending.

Twitter has become increasingly popular with organizations as a way to reach a network instantly, thus creating word-of-mouth publicity. The popular tweets are limited in length to 140 characters, making their messages succinct and pithy. When tweets are sent out to an established network, their messages are potentially viewed instantly by thousands and thousands of readers, making the potential impact invaluable.

Companies use Twitter for more than sending out tweets. An organization's Twitter page is another way for the company to present a professional image of itself. The Twitter page should include a logo or some other form of image associated with the organization; branding imagery; name and location; and a tightly worded message that embodies the organization's ethos. This short company bio embodies the Godiva chocolate brand and message:

> *Godiva Chocolatier, Inc., is the leading manufacturer of premium-quality chocolates sold worldwide. #GODIVA*

Because tweets are limited by length, they share certain characteristics, listed in Table 8.2.

Facebook

Another social media tool that has gained popularity as a public relations vehicle is the social network page, with Facebook the current favorite. Social networking sites should be considered complementary to an organization's online identity, not a replacement for it. Some consider the sites to be information gathering tools to measure marketing efforts rather than messaging tools—Facebook, for example, offers organizations considerable tools to measure involvement.

Table 8.2 Characteristics of microblogs

No headline
Profile picture or company logo or photo of an individual's face or a product, subject to change if one doesn't produce results
Casual style but grammatically correct and well edited
Questions to prompt engagement
Length of up to 140 characters or roughly 12 words
Truncated language that omits articles (*a, an, the*) and abbreviations
Link to a recommended URL using a URL shortener such as Bitly
Clearly written content containing response to another tweet, a recommendation, or link to an item of interest
Hashtags relevant to the topic
Punctuation marks "!" and "?"
Writing style similar to news headlines using action-oriented language and keywords to communicate main point

Facebook pages allow organizations to supplement their online presence by engendering interactivity among *fans* or readers. Organizations use this free new media to keep a community engaged as well as to drive traffic to their websites. Facebook pages also help brand an organization and are yet another way to communicate with stakeholders. They mirror blogs and tweets in that they, too, are conversational, interactive, and provide pertinent information to readers. Groups manage their Facebook pages by regularly updating wall posts written for news feed optimization. Essentially this means that the content encourages fans to *like* or post comments. The more *likes* a posting receives, the more liable it is that Facebook's algorithm will pick up the post and put it in a news feed. When that happens, more readers will receive the post, theoretically increasing the audience. Comments or *likes* posted on Facebook pages also help an organization gauge what's going right—or wrong!

When composing an organization's Facebook pages, public relations writers should use branding language consistent with the organization's other social media and corporate communications and stay on message.

Notice how the Santa Barbara School of Performing Arts posts information on its Facebook page in the screenshot shown in Figure 8.2.

Figure 8.2 Santa Barbara School of Performing Arts Facebook

Address your audience directly and provide information they will find entertaining or useful. Include links to relevant videos, and update the company status on a regular basis. Remember to provide information at least 80 percent of the time and to push a product or idea only 10 to 20 percent of the time.

Once the Facebook page is active, it will likely (and hopefully!) induce comments. However, not all these comments will be positive. When responding to negative remarks on Facebook (or any social media), follow these pointers:

- Act immediately. Never ignore a negative post; you'll appear disconnected.
- Contact the naysayer privately and politely. Try to "make it right" with the individual and address the problem one on one.
- Consider asking the individual to remove the post. The only time this is appropriate is if you were able to rectify the problem.

- Keep the original post. Don't remove negative messages; your community expects some negative comments and will appreciate seeing your response.

Sometimes all your best efforts will not net a happy resolution. If the individual is blatantly hostile or writes offensive epithets, ban that person from your page. Doing so is a last resort but a necessary one.

Social Media News Releases

Social media news releases differ from traditional news releases in that they are packed with multimedia. While they convey facts about a news event, they do so by listing the items in bulleted points. Social media news releases target bloggers and online journalists instead of the mainstream media. Because the audience is part of a social network, experts suggest that these types of news releases be shared with the smallest, most interested part of a network. The elements to include in a social media news release are summarized in Table 8.3.

Table 8.3 Elements of social media news release

Date, time of post
Text single spaced, double spaced between paragraphs
Headline in **boldface**; subhead that supports main news in headline (optional)
Images to download
Bulleted facts
Quotation from a notable individual within the organization
Embedded video or other media and buttons for sharing content
Contact information (name, title, e-mail, phone)
Boilerplate paragraph (About XYZ Corp.)

The sample in Figure 8.3 illustrates the basic components of a social media news release. Note how a blogger or online journalist would have very few questions about the event and could therefore write it up with ease—always your goal as a public relations practitioner!

Santa Barbara School of Performing Arts Stages *Anything Goes* at Marjorie Luke Theatre

March 11, 2017, 2:00 p.m.

News Facts

- The Santa Barbara School of Performing Arts will present Broadway classic *Anything Goes* at the Marjorie Luke Theatre
- Evening shows: Friday and Saturday, April 11 and 12 at 7 p.m.
- Matinees: Saturday and Sunday, April 12 and 13 at 1:00 p.m.
- Cast includes student actors ages 10–15
- Directed by Jessica Loden
- Musical direction by Dauri Knight
- Tickets available at Marjorie Luke Theatre Box Office; Adults $10, Children and Students, $5

Quotations

- "This Tony-award winning show highlights our talented students in Cole Porter's classic Broadway hit."

  —Jessica Loden, Co-Owner, Santa Barbara School of Performing Arts
- "We stress technique that helps build our children emotionally, physically, and intellectually."

  —Dauri Knight, Co-Owner and Musical Director, Santa Barbara School of Performing Arts

Related Links

- Santa Barbara School of Performing Arts
- The Marjorie Luke Theatre

About Santa Barbara School of Performing Arts

SBSOPA offers pre-professional training for area youth ages 5–21. Founded in 2012 by Jessica Loden and Dauri Knight, SBSOPA offers three tracks determined by audition and age.

For More Information

Jessica Loden

Director, SBSOPA

XXX@XXX.com

(555)555-5432

Figure 8.3 Sample social media news release

Conclusion

Social media has become essential for an organization's online presence. Organizations using social media must track postings, respond to inquiries, delete damaging or inflammatory comments, and post regularly, making its management time-consuming. Writing clearly with the organization's goals and values in mind is important to all social media messages. The employee adept at using social media will be a valuable member of any organization.

APPENDIX

Sample Documents

CHAPTER 2

Sample Routine E-mail

To:	Haley Kalekian <kalekian@goodmanners.com>
From:	Marsha Gulavsky <marshag@importium.com>
Date:	January 7, 2017
Cc:	
Bcc:	
Subject:	Provide Intercultural Etiquette Workshop in April?

Dear Ms. Kalekian:

Could Good Manners provide a workshop on proper etiquette for dealing with intercultural businesspeople to 50 employees the week of April 4?

I was told of your excellent professional conduct seminars by Lucille Strong at PR Pros, and I am hoping you can tailor your content to meet our needs. We want to prepare our workforce for meeting with clients from Asia, who are visiting our facility April 16. Specifically I would appreciate answers to the questions below.

1. Can you deliver the seminar or workshop at our facilities in Evanston? We have a room with an overhead projector, smart board, and lectern with hookups to most devices.
2. Would our staff have access to the materials you use after the presentation?
3. Could you provide mock situations we could videotape?

Your answers to these questions by February 15 will help me present my recommendations to our management committee.

Sincerely,
Marsha Gulavsky
Training Manager
Importium Industries

Sample Letter

JMR Public Relations

2930 Shattuck Avenue
Berkeley, CA 94705
510.936.4900
jmrpr.com

February 5, 2017

Mr. Gary Berg, Assistant Director
Holistic Healing
6643 Byland Avenue, Suite 300
Oakland, CA 94602

Dear Mr. Berg:

Thank you for choosing JMR Public Relations to represent Holistic Healing in its marketing and public relations efforts. We are confident our plans will effectively boost Holistic Healing's visibility in the booming alternative medicine arena.

Enclosed are two copies of the marketing representation agreement, which include the revised public relations and social media plan schedules we discussed on the phone today. Please sign both copies of the agreement and return them, along with the retainer mentioned in Section II, Point A, no later than February 10 so that we can meet the aggressive deadlines we have set. We will return an executed copy to you as soon as we receive your signed agreements.

We look forward to working closely with you and the rest of the Holistic Healing team over the next year.

Sincerely,

Rich Gold

Richard Gold, President
JMR Public Relations

Sample Memo

JMR Public Relations

MEMO

Date: February 5, 2017

To: Manny Doran, Media Services Manager
Elizabeth Dowley, Creative Director

From: Rich Gold, President

Subject: Holistic Healing Account and Scheduling

Now that we have landed the Holistic Healing account, we need to focus our energies on meeting the aggressive deadlines set in the contract. Below are the two main areas on which we should concentrate.

Relationship Building

To foster goodwill and build strong working relationships, we should set up a series of meetings and lunches in which our key people meet with the Holistic Healing team. Be sure your staff goes into these meetings fully armed with research and knowledge about this market so that when they spend time at the site, they can better absorb details. This is a new arena for us, and we need to get up to speed quickly.

Branding or Media Plan

By March, we should be working on creative approaches to bring to the client by the end of the month. That will include recommendations for:

- Print and online media with CPM estimates
- Social media strategy: Blog, Facebook, Instagram, etc.
- Branding
- Storyboards, print ad, and online ads

Please send me a progress report detailing your plans to meet these goals by noon on Thursday, February 11. This will be a busy few months, but I'm certain your teams are up to the task.

Sample Negative News Letter

HAPPY VALLEY HISTORICAL SOCIETY
52 HILLVIEW DRIVE   HAPPY VALLEY, OR 97015
(503) 356-9954   WWW.HVHISTORY.COM

February 5, 2017

Mrs. Margaret Sangford
11 Park Drive
Happy Valley, OR 97015

Dear Mrs. Sangford:

Thank you for your well researched proposal to include Mayweather House in this year's *Giving Back!*® volunteer day. Mayweather House's distinctive architectural style and garden is indeed one that merits preservation for future generations.

As you may be aware, our primary goal is to improve homes in our town's most neglected areas. We gave close consideration to the 22 submissions we received and were able to include the 10 homes in the most dire condition for this year's rehabilitation efforts. While Mayweather House was not one of the selected properties, we encourage you to apply again next year.

We are grateful that citizens like you take the effort to support our ongoing efforts to improve our town and share your commitment to bring Happy Valley's architectural gems back to their original glory.

Sincerely,

Annabel McElmurray
Annabel McElmurray
Public Relations Manager

CHAPTER 4

Sample News Release

SANTA BARBARA
School of
Performing
Arts

Contact ··
Contact: Jessica Loden
555.123.4567
jloden@sbsopa.com

Headline ·············
**Santa Barbara School of Performing Arts
Stages *Anything Goes* at Marjorie Luke Theatre**

Dateline ·····
Lead ········
SANTA BARBARA, CA (March 11, 2017)--The Santa Barbara School of Performing Arts will
present the Broadway classic Anything Goes at the Marjorie Luke Theatre April 11-13.

The cast, comprised of student actors ages 10-15, will perform evening shows on Friday
and Saturday at 7:00 p.m. and matinees on Saturday and Sunday at 1:00 pm.

"This Tony-award winning show highlights our talented students in Cole Porter's classic
Broadway hit," said Jessica Loden, co-owner SBSOPA and the show's director.

Santa Barbara School of Performing Arts offers pre-professional training for area youth
ages 5-21. Founded in 2012 by Jessica Loden and Dauri Knight, SBSOPA's conservatory
program is designed to nurture, motivate, and build confidence in the community's
youth through the use of contemporary and classic musical theatre. The group offers
three tracks. Performers are placed after auditioning and by age.

Anything Goes is the organization's third show and features many well-known musical
numbers including "I Get a Kick Out of You" and "You're the Top."

"We stress technique that helps build our children emotionally, physically, and intellectually," said Dauri Knight, SBSOPA co-owner and musical director of the show.

Tickets may be purchased at the Marjorie Luke Theatre Box office or online at
www.marjorieluke.com. For more information, please contact Jessica Loden at
jloden@sbsopa.com or phone (XXX-XXX-XXXX.)

Boilerplate ···
About Santa Barbara School for Performing Arts. SBSOPA, a 501(c)3 non-profit
organization, offers pre-professional voice and theatrical training for area youth ages
5-21. Funded by grants and community donations, the organization's goal is to turn
away no child with a desire to participate. For more information, visit www.sbsopa.com.

Endmark ··   # # #

CHAPTER 6

Sample Pitch Letter

April 13, 2017

Mr. John Doe
Staff Writer
Travel on a Budget
11111 Park Place
New York, NY 10001

Dear Mr. Doe:

Brad Smith and his buddies are such hardcore campers that they plan their monthly weekend getaways a year in advance. But after repeatedly visiting the same old location near their homes in San Diego, they needed a new spot. The guys were pretty picky, though. Brad insisted on pristine hiking trails. Mario needed clear streams with plenty of fish. They all wanted rugged bicycle paths and untouched natural surroundings. Then Brad found Idyllwild. And things got a little, well, wild! Did I mention the bear? Never mind, the story has a happy ending.

I think readers of Travel on a Budget would enjoy hearing about the camping adventures of Brad and his friends in the little-known gem of Idyllwild, California. Nestled halfway between Los Angeles and San Diego in the San Jacinto Mountains, Idyllwild gave these working men a weekend they'll not soon forget. Such an article would complement your recent series on weekend getaways in Northern California and would appeal to active readers who want to learn about affordable destinations with lots of exciting activities.

We can offer you this story as an exclusive and provide you with access to Brad and his colorful camping cohorts as well as exquisite still and video footage of Idyllwild's natural surroundings, but I'd have to know your intention by [date]. We can even give you a shot of Brad and the bear! Please give me a call at 555-111-1234 or email me at xxx@xxx.com to let me know if I can be of any help.

I'll follow up with you on [date] to see how I might be able to assist you. Thanks for your consideration.

Sincerely,

Your Name
[Name, Position]

Notes

Chapter 2

1. Feintzeig (2014).
2. Alred, Brusaw, and Oliu (2014, 47).
3. Guffey and Loewy (2015, 207).
4. Martin (2014).
5. Alred, Brusaw, and Oliu (2014, 49).
6. Guffey and Loewy (2013, 108).
7. "Nine Steps to More Effective Business Emails" (2013).
8. "Nine Steps to More Effective Business Emails" (2013).
9. Covey (2012, 145).

Chapter 3

1. Hoffman (2014).
2. Bank of America (2015).
3. PR Newswire (2014).

Chapter 4

1. Diggs-Brown (2013, 121).
2. Smith (2014).

Chapter 6

1. Diggs-Brown (2013, 64).
2. Diggs-Brown (2013, 62).
3. Marsh, Guth, and Short (2005, 51).

Chapter 7

1. Barton, Kalmbach, and Lowe (2011, 4).

2. Nielsen (1997).

3. Nielsen (2006).

4. Nielsen (1997).

5. Nielsen (2010).

6. Redish (2012, 54).

7. Redish (2012, 30).

8. Nielsen (2000, 101).

Chapter 8

1. Intel (2015).

2. Eadicicco (2015).

3. Maltby (2013).

References

Alred, G.J., C.T. Brusaw, and W. Oliu. 2014. *The Business Writer's Companion.* 7th ed. Boston, MA: Bedford St. Martin's.

Bank of America. 2015. *World's Top Professional Wheelchair Athletes Compete This Fall in 2015 Chicago-New York Challenge in Preview of New Abbott World Marathon Majors Series.* [Press Release]. Retrieved from http://newsroom. bankofamerica.com/press-releases/community/worlds-top-professional-wheelchair-athletes-compete-fall-2015-chicago-new-y

Barton, M., J. Kalmbach, and C. Lowe, eds. 2011. *Writing Spaces. Web Writing Style Guide Version 1.0.* Anderson, SC: Parlor Press, LLC.

Covey, S. 2012. *Style Guide for Business and Technical Communication.* 5th ed. Upper Saddle River, NJ: FT Press.

Diggs-Brown, B. 2013. *The PR Style Guide.* 3rd ed. Boston, MA: Cengage Learning.

Eadicicco, L. May 30, 2015. "Google Just Showed Us Where It's Miles Ahead of Apple." Business Insider. Retrieved from www.businessinsider.com/google-machine-learning-miles-ahead-of-apple-2015-5 (accessed August 15, 2015).

Feintzeig, R. 2014. "A Company Without Email? Not So Fast." *The Wall Street Journal,* June 17, www.wsj.com/articles/a-company-without-email-not-so-fast-1403048134 (accessed August 13, 2015).

Guffey, M., and D. Loewy. 2013. *Essentials of Business Communication.* 9th ed. Mason, OH: South-Western Cengage Learning.

Guffey, M., and D. Loewy. 2015. *Business Communication, Process and Product.* 8th ed. Stamford, CT: Cengage Learning.

Hoffman, A. 2014. *Press Release Boot Camp: What You Need to Know.* PR Newswire Association. http://promotions.prnewswire.com/rs/prnewswire/images/N-CO-2.2.1_Press_Release_Checklist.pdf

Intel. 2015. "Social Media Guidelines." Intel.com. Retrieved from www.intel.com/content/www/us/en/legal/intel-social-media-guidelines.html (accessed August 15, 2015).

Maltby, E. January 31, 2013. "Some Social-Media Tips for Business Owners." Onlinewsj.com. Retrieved from http://live.wsj.com/video/social-media-tips-for-small-businesses/1688579B-EA7C-4C6A-B16B-4369A053F50A.html?KEYWORDS=emily+maltby#!1688579B-EA7C-4C6A-B16B-4369A053F50A (accessed August 13, 2015).

Marsh, C., D. Guth, and B. Short. 2005. *Strategic Writing: Multimedia Writing for Public Relations, Advertising, Sales and Marketing*. Boston, MA: Pearson Education.

Martin, E. 2014. "The 12 Most Common Email Mistakes Professionals Make." BusinessInsider.com www.businessinsider.com/common-email-mistakes-professionals-make-2014-7 (accessed August 13, 2015).

Nielsen, J. October 1, 1997. "How Users Read on the Web." Useit.com. Retrieved from www.useit.com/alertbox/9710a.html (accessed August 13, 2015).

Nielsen, J. 2000. *Designing Web Usability*. Indianapolis, IN: New Riders Publishing.

Nielsen, J. April 17, 2006. "F-Shaped Pattern for Reading Web Content." Useit.com. Retrieved from www.useit.com/alertbox/reading_pattern.html (accessed August 13, 2015).

Nielsen, J. April 6, 2010. "Horizontal Attention Leans Left." Useit.com. Retrieved from www.useit.com/alertbox/horizontal-attention.html (accessed August 13, 2015).

"Nine Steps to More Effective Business Emails." October 15, 2013. A Blog for the Comma Man. http://freestyle-blog.com/2013/10/15/nine-steps-to-more-effective-business-emails/ (accessed August 13, 2015).

PR Newswire. 2014. "Quick and Easy Guide to Sharing Your Press Release with the World." PR Newswire. http://promotions.prnewswire.com/rs/prnewswire/images/E-CO-1.4.2_Quick_and_Easy_Guide_to_Getting_Your_Press_Release_on_the_Wire.pdf (accessed August 13, 2015).

Redish, J. 2012. *Letting Go of the Word: Writing Web Content that Works*. Waltham, MA: Elsevier Inc.

Smith, L. October 15, 2014. "Best Practices for Emails+ Why They Are Important." Litmus.com [blog]. https://litmus.com/blog/best-practices-for-plain-text-emails-a-look-at-why-theyre-important (accessed August 13, 2015).

Index

OTHER TITLES IN OUR CORPORATE COMMUNICATION COLLECTION

Debbie DuFrene, Stephen F. Austin State University, Editor

- *Web Content: A Writer's Guide* by Janet Mizrahi
- *SPeak Performance: Using the Power of Metaphors to Communicate Vision, Motivate People, and Lead Your Organization to Success* by Jim Walz
- *Today's Business Communication: A How-To Guide for the Modern Professional* by Jason L. Snyder and Robert Forbus
- *Leadership Talk: A Discourse Approach to Leader Emergence* by Robyn Walker and Jolanta Aritz
- *Communication Beyond Boundaries* by Payal Mehra
- *Managerial Communication* by Reginald L. Bell and Jeanette S. Martin
- *Writing for the Workplace: Business Communication for Professionals* by Janet Mizrahi
- *Get Along, Get It Done, Get Ahead: Interpersonal Communication in the Diverse Workplace* by Geraldine E. Hynes
- *The Language of Success: The Confidence and Ability to Say What You Mean and Mean What You Say in Business and Life* by Kim Wilkerson and Alan Weiss
- *Writing Online: A Guide to Effective Digital Communication at Work* by Erika Darics

Announcing the Business Expert Press Digital Library

Concise e-books business students need for classroom and research

This book can also be purchased in an e-book collection by your library as

- a one-time purchase,
- that is owned forever,
- allows for simultaneous readers,
- has no restrictions on printing, and
- can be downloaded as PDFs from within the library community.

Our digital library collections are a great solution to beat the rising cost of textbooks. E-books can be loaded into their course management systems or onto students' e-book readers.
The **Business Expert Press** digital libraries are very affordable, with no obligation to buy in future years. For more information, please visit **www.businessexpertpress.com/librarians**. To set up a trial in the United States, please email **sales@businessexpertpress.com**.

CPSIA information can be obtained
at www.ICGtesting.com
Printed in the USA
LVHW022106210720
661235LV00015B/1500